T0339560

Cambridge Elements ≡

Elements in Phonetics
edited by
David Deterding
Universiti Brunei Darussalam

PHONETICS AND PHONOLOGY IN MULTILINGUAL LANGUAGE DEVELOPMENT

Ulrike Gut
University of Münster

Romana Kopečková
University of Münster

Christina Nelson
University of Münster

 CAMBRIDGE
UNIVERSITY PRESS

Shaftesbury Road, Cambridge CB2 8EA, United Kingdom

One Liberty Plaza, 20th Floor, New York, NY 10006, USA

477 Williamstown Road, Port Melbourne, VIC 3207, Australia

314–321, 3rd Floor, Plot 3, Splendor Forum, Jasola District Centre, New Delhi – 110025, India

103 Penang Road, #05–06/07, Visioncrest Commercial, Singapore 238467

Cambridge University Press is part of Cambridge University Press & Assessment, a department of the University of Cambridge.

We share the University's mission to contribute to society through the pursuit of education, learning and research at the highest international levels of excellence.

www.cambridge.org
Information on this title: www.cambridge.org/9781108994743

DOI: 10.1017/9781108992527

First published 2023

A catalogue record for this publication is available from the British Library.

ISBN 978-1-108-99474-3 Paperback
ISSN 2634-1689 (online)
ISSN 2634-1670 (print)

Cambridge University Press & Assessment has no responsibility for the persistence or accuracy of URLs for external or third-party internet websites referred to in this publication and does not guarantee that any content on such websites is, or will remain, accurate or appropriate.

Phonetics and Phonology in Multilingual Language Development

Elements in Phonetics

DOI: 10.1017/9781108992527
First published online: July 2023

Ulrike Gut
University of Münster

Romana Kopečková
University of Münster

Christina Nelson
University of Münster

Author for correspondence: Ulrike Gut, gut@uni-muenster.de

Abstract: This Element focusses on phonetic and phonological development in multilinguals and presents a novel methodological approach to it within Complex Dynamic Systems Theory (CDST). We will show how the traditional conceptualisations of acquisition, with a strong focus on linear, incremental development with a stable end point, can be complemented by a view of language development as emergent, self-organised, context-dependent and highly variable across learners. We report on a longitudinal study involving sixteen learners with L1 German, L2 English and L3 Polish. Over their ten months of learning Polish, the learners' perception and production of various speech sounds and phonological processes in all of their languages were investigated. Auditory and acoustic analyses were applied together with group and individual learner statistical analyses to trace the dynamic changes of their multilingual phonological system over time. We show how phonetic and phonological development is feature-dependent and interconnected and how learning experience affects the process.

Keywords: third language acquisition, speech perception, speech production, multilingual, Complex Dynamic Systems Theory

ISBNs: 9781108994743 (PB), 9781108992527 (OC)
ISSNs: 2634-1689 (online), 2634-1670 (print)

Contents

1 Introduction

Foreign language instructors and language students are commonly fascinated by the differences between the speech of native and non-native speakers of a language. They may have their intuitions, possibly stemming from their own experiences with teaching and learning foreign languages, about the challenges involved in perceiving and producing the sounds of a new language. The scientific study of the development of perception and production of sounds in a foreign language has a seventy-year-long tradition, and numerous theoretical models as well as empirical research have yielded important insights into various factors that can influence the learning process. In the first decades of research into phonological acquisition of foreign languages, the language that was learned was usually referred to as a second language (L2), which was used as an umbrella term for all foreign languages no matter how many and when they were learned. With the important insight that not only the native language (L1) but also the other languages a speaker knows can influence the phonological acquisition of a target language, a terminological distinction has been proposed between a learner's first foreign language (L2) and their further foreign languages (L3). In this Element, we will refer to the chronologically first learned foreign language as the L2 and to languages that are learned chronologically later as the L3. L3 learners will also be referred to as multilingual learners.

The observation that a learner's multiple languages interact has been widely documented in both speech perception and production. This phenomenon, referred to as cross-linguistic influence (CLI), has been shown in the acquisition of target sounds (e.g., Amengual et al., 2019; Cabrelli & Pichan, 2019; Gabriel et al., 2016; Kopečková, 2014, 2016; Kopečková et al., 2016; Llama et al., 2010; Llama & Cardoso, 2018; Llama & López-Morelos, 2016; Morales Reyes et al., 2017; Patience, 2018; Wrembel, 2014, 2015) and prosody (e.g., Cabrelli & Rothman, 2010; Gut, 2010) as well as phonological processes (e.g., Cebrian, 2000; Sato, 1984). Related findings have also revealed that such an influence is multidirectional in nature, i.e., that it concerns not only the influence of an earlier acquired language (whether L1 or L2) on the later acquired language but also vice versa (e.g., Aoki & Nishihara, 2013; Beckmann, 2012; Cabrelli, 2016; Cabrelli & Rothman, 2010; Sypiańska, 2016, 2017). Research into L3 phonological learning has further drawn our attention to the possibility that more than one language can act as the source of this influence, i.e., a simultaneous (combined) influence of more than one language at the same time (see De Angelis, 2007; Wrembel, 2015), critically distinguishing the learning constellation of L2 learners from that of L3 learners. Multiple language knowledge thus entails an increase in the number of potential cross-linguistic interactions as well as in the number of potential directions.

Indeed, one of the main tenets of the L3 acquisition field is that learning a second foreign language is fundamentally different from learning a foreign language for the first time. It is not only the broadened phonetic repertoire and hence a potential for a range of cross-linguistic interactions but also the learner's greater experience with language learning that qualitatively distinguish the learning situations. L3 learners have already learned their first foreign language to some extent and thus are likely to have discovered their individual learning strategies and style to further their own L3 learning success (Hufeisen, 2010). Studies examining the effects of having learned a first foreign language on L3 speech perception and production have further shown that L3 learners tend to outperform L2 learners in target language phonetic discrimination and sound production, which has been explained by L3 learners' raised level of metaphonological awareness and/or enhanced perceptual sensitivity (e.g., Antoniou et al., 2015; Kopečková, 2016).

Yet one characteristic of non-native speech perception and production arguably common to L2 and L3 learners is the large amount of variability between learners (inter-learner variability) and within the same learner (intra-learner variability). The sources of such variability have been shown to be either linguistic factors, such as segmental and prosodic contexts in which the target occurs, or learner-related factors. The latter can include a myriad of learner-internal factors (e.g., age at onset of language learning, phonological awareness, motivation) as well as learner-external factors (e.g., quality and quantity of phonetic input, opportunities for language use). It has been shown that each of the learner-related factors is subject to change in the course of an individual's phonological development, and therefore definite predictions about a learner's pattern of development may be hard to make.

The goal of scientific explorations of L2/L3 phonological acquisition is to gain a systematic understanding of the processes and factors involved in the acquisition of a target sound system and to explain the perception and production outcomes observed for learners. This Element aims to contribute to this goal by presenting findings from a study that investigates the development of phonology in all of the languages of multilingual speakers across a ten-month period. It will do so based on a novel methodological approach that was developed within a relatively recent theoretical framework of foreign language development: Complex Dynamic Systems Theory (CDST) (de Bot et al., 2007; Larsen-Freeman & Cameron, 2008; Verspoor et al., 2011).

In Sections 2 and 3, we review the state of the art with regard to L2 and L3 phonological acquisition. Section 2 presents and compares the currently leading theories of L2 speech learning. We will discuss the extent to which the L2 theories offer suitable frameworks with respect to modelling phonological learning by multilingual speakers, i.e., speakers who speak and learn several foreign languages at the same time. Section 3 explains that the traditional conceptualisations of phonological acquisition which underlie both previous research and the theories presented in Section 2 tend to imply that foreign language speech learning is a linear, incremental process with a stable end point. It then presents Complex Dynamic Systems Theory, which conceptualises language development as an emergent, self-organised process with high variability across learners. It goes on to show which new methodologies are used to investigate foreign language phonological development within this framework. Section 4 presents the methodology of our longitudinal study involving sixteen learners with L1 German, L2 English and L3 Polish. The results are presented in Section 5 and discussed in Section 6. The Element concludes with suggestions for possible directions in future research in the area of L2/L3 phonological acquisition.

2 Theories of L2 Phonological Acquisition

It is widely recognised that L2 speakers normally sound different from L1 speakers of the target language. Although an intuitive account of this could lead one to believe that this is primarily due to production difficulties that affect L2 learners' performance, most theories of L2 speech learning assume that the learners' difficulty to produce target language sounds is actually perceptual in nature, i.e., that it is directly linked to the learners' ability to detect similarities and differences between the sounds of their L1 and the sounds of their L2. Languages differ in their contrastive phonemes (e.g., English and Polish have /w/ and /v/ while German only has /v/), but phonemes may also vary across languages in terms of their phonetic properties (e.g., German /v/ is produced differently from English and Polish /v/). Theories of L2 speech learning describe, predict and explain L2 difficulty based on their particular view regarding the phonological and/or phonetic properties of the learners' L1 categories (i.e., long-term memory representation of sounds) in comparison to L2 sound categories.

Two perception-based models have inspired the majority of L2 perception and production studies conducted on a variety of first language and target language combinations, namely the Perceptual Assimilation Model (PAM: Best, 1995; and PAM-L2: Best & Tyler, 2007) and the Speech Learning Model (SLM: Flege, 1995, 2003; and SLM-r: Flege & Bohn, 2021). While the former aims to explain the development of foreign speech perception at both the phonetic and the phonological level, the latter model aspires to address both the perception and the production development in an L2 at the phonetic level. Both models were developed to predict the influence of an L1 onto an L2 and have so far not been expanded to include potential influences of any additional languages on the learner's perceptual mappings of the target sounds.

Best's Perceptual Assimilation Model (PAM: Best, 1995) and its adaptation to L2 speech learning (PAM-L2: Best & Tyler, 2007; Tyler, 2019) propose that the learner's ability to perceive L2 sound contrasts depends on the degree to which L2 sounds are assimilated to the exemplars of L1 sound categories. It follows a *direct realist* or ecological approach to speech perception that argues that listeners detect speech information in terms of articulatory gestures such as the manner and place of articulation rather than on the basis of any mental representation of sounds (Best, 1995; Fowler, 1986). In other words, the L2 learner engages in perceptually assimilating the articulatory gestures of target sounds to the articulatory gestures of their L1 phonemes. A non-native sound can be heard as a good or a poor example of an L1 phoneme (*categorised*), as different from any particular L1 phoneme (*uncategorised*) or as a non-speech sound (*non-assimilated*). Accordingly, different pairwise assimilation types associated with different levels of L2 discrimination difficulty have been proposed in the model (for a description of all assimilation types and their predictions, see Tyler, 2021).

For example, both sounds of an L2 contrast can be judged as members of a single L1 sound category. When both members of the non-native contrast are phonetically and phonologically perceived as good or poor members of a single L1 category (single-category assimilation), then the discrimination in the L2 will be very poor. An example for such a scenario for German learners of Polish might be Polish /w/ and /v/ (as in *łata* /wata/ 'patch' and *wata* /vata/ 'cotton wool'), both of which may be perceived as members of the German category /v/ and therefore poorly discriminated at the beginning of L2 learning. However, if one sound of the contrast is perceived as a much poorer member of the L1 category than the other (category-goodness assimilation), then discrimination between these two non-native sounds may range from moderate to very good, depending on how dissimilar the two non-native sounds are from the L1 sound category (Shinohara et al., 2019). The PAM-L2 predicts that, with increasing L2 experience, new L2 categories can be formed as a result of the learner's growing L2 lexicon when noticing that there are minimally contrasting words in the target language that are communicatively relevant. As will be explained in Section 4, an interesting learning constellation arises in this connection for German learners of Polish as an L3 and English as an L2. For these experienced language learners, the /v-w/ contrast is shared in both of their foreign languages;

if acquired in the L2 as a result of the category-goodness assimilation there is a potential for a facilitative phonetic mapping of the contrast from the learners' L2 onto their L3 categories rather than non-facilitation stemming from their L1 (an interaction with L2 and L3 orthography has to be further considered in this specific case).

Another possible pattern for discrimination of L2 contrasts occurs when one member of the contrast is perceived as a member of an L1 category and one is perceived as uncategorisable (categorised-uncategorised assimilation). Such an L2 contrast should be discriminated well because it reflects a phonological distinction between an exemplar of a known phoneme and an unknown sound. However, this type can be discriminated poorly when the uncategorised sound is in close phonological space to the categorised sound (Faris et al., 2016). A possible sound contrast that may fit this pattern for German learners of Polish is Polish /ɛ/ and /ɛ̃/ (as in *step* /stɛp/ 'steppe' and *stęp* /stɛ̃p/ 'gait') since the Polish nasal vowel is probably perceived as uncategorisable by many L1 German speakers.

The PAM-L2 uses these PAM assimilation types to predict the likelihood of category formation for L2 sounds when an L2 learner (rather than a naive listener/beginner L2 learner in the case of the PAM) is actively using the target language. Perceptual discrimination should thus improve when the assimilation type changes as a result of new category acquisition (e.g., a single-category assimilation becomes a category-goodness assimilation), the prerequisite being that the learner is exposed to input that preserves phonetic differences. Tyler (2019) explains that in classroom settings, in contrast to an immersion environment with rich native speaker input, teachers who speak the target language as an L2 may fail to provide clear phonetic differences between L2 categories and thus inhibit the likelihood of their learners' L2 category acquisition. The outcome is not necessarily to be linked to the teacher not being a native speaker though, as accented speech may also preserve the phonological distinction between all L2 phonemes and thus facilitate the learner's formation of relevant L2 categories. Similarly, written language input, which constitutes probably the main difference between immersion and classroom L2 acquisition, may reinforce the perception of L2 categories as based on L1 grapheme-phoneme correspondences and thus hinder L2 category formation. Finally, Tyler (2019) elaborates on the effect of prior foreign language exposure (i.e., target language exposure) on perception learning, which has a special relevance for the predictions of the PAM-L2. For instance, a learner with previous exposure to the L2 may have already established a category-goodness contrast as a single L1–L2 category and therefore their perceptual learning trajectory may be set before classroom exposure. This may happen, for example, when a learner previously learned to read the L2 and, in the absence of spoken input, applied their L1 phonology to a considerable amount of L2 words via orthography (Tyler, 2019, p. 617). The presence of previous language exposure can therefore hamper the prediction of category acquisition. In any case, it is conceivable that L2 phonemes included in the single-category assimilation type and the category-goodness assimilation type will be even more difficult to acquire in the classroom setting, whereas the acquisition of the uncategorised L2 phonemes in turn may be supported in such a learning environment, especially where L2 orthography is present and provides an unambiguous distinction.

As stated, neither the PAM nor the PAM-L2 make specific predictions regarding the development of speech perception by L3 learners, i.e., those with prior foreign language exposure to additional languages. In one of the rare studies that extended the predictions of the PAM-L2 to the context of multilingual phonological acquisition, Wrembel et al. (2019) found that multilinguals assimilate L3 vowel sounds to both L1 and L2 categories with a preference for the latter, at least in their population of L1 German, L2 English and L3 Polish learners. The study also showed that even beginner L3 learners formed new L3 categories, distinguishing between highly similar L3 sibilant pairs that would typically follow the single-category assimilation pattern. In other words, in terms of perceptual acquisition, beginner L3 learners were argued to behave similarly to advanced L2 learners in that they were able to discriminate sound contrasts predicted by the PAM-L2 to be challenging.

Unlike the PAM/PAM-L2, which assumes that perceivers extract speech information at a gestural/articulatory level, Flege's Speech Learning Model (SLM: Flege, 1995, 2002, 2003) and its revised version (SLM-r: Flege & Bohn, 2021) assume that perceivers form a long-term mental representation for target sounds from acoustic-phonetic cues. According to the SLM/SLM-r, this is a learning mechanism that is involved in L1 speech learning and that remains intact throughout life. Yet monolingual-like performance is not expected on the part of L2 learners as their L1 and L2 categories are stored in the common phonological space, inevitably influencing each other (Flege, 1995, 2002; referred to as 'common phonetic space' in Flege & Bohn, 2021). This regularly leads to *category assimilation* in which L1 and L2 sounds of the learner are perceptually equated; a target language category is blocked and a composite or *merged L1–L2 category* is then used to perceive and produce both the L2 and the L1 sounds, leading to bidirectional cross-linguistic influence. Consequently, the model predicts that learners who have a merged L1–L2 category will not display monolingual-like performance as they are likely to produce sounds differently from monolinguals of either language.

One of the main hypotheses of the SLM/SLM-r is that the greater the perceived dissimilarity between L1 and L2 sounds, the greater the likelihood that learners establish target-like categories and consequently perceive and produce the target sounds more accurately. However, similar L2 sounds may remain difficult to learn, as L2 learners might not be able to discern the subtle phonetic differences between the L2 and L1 sounds and thus they will readily map the target sounds onto L1 categories, perceiving and producing such L2 sounds in terms of those L1 categories. For example, German learners of Polish are likely to easily detect the phonetic differences between the rhotic sounds of their L1 and L2, the uvular fricative /ʁ/ and alveolar trill /r/, respectively. Although the Polish rhotic may be initially difficult to produce, the likelihood of L2 category formation for such a novel sound is predicted in the model to be high. In contrast, the subtle phonetic differences and complex acoustic cues applied in distinguishing between word-final voiced and voiceless obstruents may be a particular learning challenge for German learners of English because they can be expected to apply their voiceless L1 category (in this word-final position) in perceiving and producing the target obstruents. It is to be noted in this regard that the position of the target language categories within a word is highly relevant, i.e., whether an individual sound occurs in the initial, medial or final position. According to the model, it is at the level of position-sensitive allophones that L1 and L2 categories are compared and refined with experience.

Similarly to the PAM-L2, the SLM/SLM-r assumes a continuous, slow refinement of L2 learners' perception of phonetic differences between their L1 and L2 as a function of the quality and quantity of phonetic input obtained in meaningful communication. For instance, Flege and Liu (2001) showed that, for two groups of L2 learners who resided in the target language country for the same amount of time (i.e., as measured by length of residence), it was only the students and not the age-matched learners in other occupations who showed improvement towards native-like performance. The authors argued that the student group was exposed to a substantially greater amount of native-like L2 input, which enhanced their identification of word-final consonants.

In the original SLM, the ability to form new phonetic categories for an L2 sound was further predicted to be mediated by the age (of onset) of L2 speech learning. Adult (late) L2 learners were predicted in the model to readily subsume L2 sounds into L1 categories thanks to the assimilative power of their well-established L1 sound categories, thus failing to form new categories for some L2 sounds. Child (early) learners, in contrast, were predicted to be less influenced by their evolving L1 sound system, and thereby more likely to form separate categories for L2 sounds and thus to learn the target language sounds to native-like levels. Considering the generality of this hypothesis and mainly the difficulty of disentangling the development of the L1 sound system from the overall state of neurocognitive development of child L2 learners, the revised version of the model (SLM-r) replaces the 'age hypothesis' with the 'L1 precision hypothesis'. According to this hypothesis, the more precise the L1 category when L2 learning begins, the more likely the phonetic differences between L1 and L2 sounds will be discerned and a new L2 category formed. In this connection, Flege and Bohn (2021) point out that individual differences in L1 category precision apply to all age groups and are potentially linked to auditory acuity, early-stage (pre-categorical) auditory processing and auditory working memory. The authors call for future research to evaluate the role of L1 category precision in L2 speech development, also with respect to the question of whether individual differences in L1 category precision affect how much L2 input learners need in order to show consistent patterns of interlingual identification.

Also, the SLM-r no longer focusses primarily on examining highly proficient L2 learners but instead acknowledges that it is the early stages of L2 development that offer an insight into the process of L2 phonetic category formation because it is only then that cross-linguistic measures of dissimilarity can serve as a predictor of later-formed L2 categories. It is likely that, with increasing L2 experience, perceived phonetic dissimilarity between L1 and L2 sounds will grow.

Another major hypothesis of the SLM/SLM-r concerns the link between the development of L2 sound perception and production. In the original version of the model, accurate L2 sound perception was predicted to be a precondition for accurate L2 sound production. Based on the observation of inconsistencies in related L2 research, the SLM-r also revises this hypothesis and proposes that L2 segmental perception and production co-evolve without precedence, i.e., that there exists a strong bidirectional connection between the two modalities although 'the correspondence between the two is never perfect, even in monolinguals' (Flege & Bohn, 2021, p. 19).

Finally, the SLM-r makes a fundamental move in orientation from examining between-group differences towards analysing the learning trajectories of individual L2 learners. Because L1 speakers cannot be all assumed to have formed the very same L1 categories (e.g., Hillebrand et al., 1995), their L1–L2 mappings and consequently L2 speech learning trajectories and outcomes will vary (e.g., Escudero & Williams, 2012). Also, Flege and Bohn (2021, p. 38) admit that two practicalities motivated their call for this methodological shift in L2 speech research: the difficulty to constitute groups differing in one variable only and the challenge to always be able to draw meaningful generalisations from group data. Future L2 research conducted within the SLM-r framework should therefore refocus on individual L2 learners and adapt its research design accordingly, i.e., 'obtaining enough data from each participant to permit treating each individual as a separate experiment' (p. 38). Section 3 explains this more specifically and suggests what research designs and statistical analyses may be most conducive to such a new agenda in L2/L3 phonology research.

In summary, the PAM/PAM-L2 and the SLM/SLM-r relate the development of perception and production abilities in an L2 to the perception of cross-language (dis)similarity. Specifically, the PAM/PAM-L2 proposes that L2 contrasts that are phonetically and phonologically assimilated to a single L1 category will be the most challenging for the L2 learners to perceive, whereas the SLM/SLM-r contends that L2 sounds (rather than contrasts) that are perceived as phonetically similar to L1 sounds will be perceived and produced in terms of those L1 categories, and thus be the most challenging to achieve. Both models propose that L2 learners (children and adults alike) will never show monolingual-like performance because L1 and L2 categories coexist in the same phonological space. The models also agree that L2 learners can improve in their L2 speech learning as a result of rich and relevant L2 phonetic input. The models diverge in their explanation of the processes involved in L2 speech learning. Whereas the PAM/PAM-L2 posits that L2 learners extract information about articulatory gestures from the speech signal, the SLM/SLM-r focusses on the development of phonetic categories from acoustic-phonetic cues. Likewise, the models dis-agree on the linkage between perception and production: while the PAM-L2 postulates no direct link between perception and production (Tyler, 2019, p. 619), the SLM-r proposes a co-evolution of the two modalities. Finally, the new goal of the SLM-r is to account for how individual L2 learners reorganise their phonetic system over time in response to the phonetic input received.

Apart from perception-based models explaining the learning trajectory of L2 learners, theoretical models that focus on various aspects of acquiring L2 speech production have also been advanced (e.g., Eckman, 1981; Lado, 1957; Major, 2002). Although this theorising is less prominent in present research into L2 phonetic and phonological acquisition, one production-based model seems relevant for its developmental perspective on the process of L2 speech learning: Major's (2001, 2002) Ontogeny and Phylogeny Model (OPM) posits that L2 speech learning is influenced by a learner's L1, L2 and certain universal processes common to language learning and human language in general. One example of such a universal process is final obstruent devoicing (e.g., *bed* pronounced as [bet]), a phonological process resulting in a less *marked* struc-ture: voiceless codas are unmarked in comparison to their voiced counterparts in that the former could be understood as 'simpler'. Various criteria have been proposed to determine which structures are less marked, including implicational universals (i.e., 'if A then B', but not the other way around), how frequently the structure occurs across languages and the order in which children acquire the structure in their L1.

The OPM proposes an initial dominant influence of the L1 in L2 speech learning, the emergent influence of universals and finally the possibility of target-like L2 speech production, especially for structures dissimilar to L1 and for less marked structures. Interestingly, Major (2001) claims that the model is equally valid for multilinguals, for whom 'L1' can be replaced by 'L1 plus L2/L3/Ln'. However, there is no proposal in the model for either the mechanisms that trigger the influence of L1 (and L2) and universals or the role of input in L2/L3 speech development.

At present, there is no model of speech learning from a multilingual perspective, largely because of our scarce knowledge about the concurrent phonological development in a multilingual speaker's different languages. The aim of this Element is therefore to contribute to the investigation of multilingual phonological development with new data, including all languages of the multilingual speakers, both adolescents and adults, and in terms of both their speech perception and production. We will trace the interaction of a range of phonological features and of individual speakers' languages with a view of offering new insights into the L3 speech learning process.

3 The Conceptualisation of Foreign Language Development

3.1 Implied Concepts in Models of Foreign Language Development and Research Methods

In early models of and research on L2 phonological acquisition, the language acquisition process was generally implied to be linear, leading from a starting point or initial phase of no knowledge of the target language to an end point, the final outcome of acquisition. This holds true for all early models and conceptualisations of L2 acquisition (as reviewed, e.g., by Colantoni et al., 2015, pp. 14–16), which were implicitly based on the assumption that the L2 acquisition process shares the linear development of successive stages that had been proposed as a universal process in L1 acquisition. Accordingly, L2 acquisition has often been modelled as a 'progression' (Saville-Troike, 2006, p. 18; Sharwood-Smith, 1999, p. 32) of successive and often predictable stages leading to a stable end point.

For L2 phonological acquisition, these theoretical assumptions are implicitly made in all models discussed in Section 2. For example, the OPM (Major, 2001) predicts that, in the initial stage of phonological acquisition, CLI from the L1 is most extensive and target language structures non-existent. In later stages, the relationship is reversed with L1 properties losing their impact and phonological properties of the target language increasingly appearing. Likewise, the SLM/ SLM-r (Flege, 1995; Flege & Bohn, 2021) views phonological acquisition as a process in which L1 phonetic features and their representations initially constrain an L2 speaker's perception and production of the target sounds. This can be overcome by achieving specific L2 speech learning 'landmarks' (Flege & Bohn, 2021, p. 38), such as the use of target-like cue-weighting in the perception of an L2 sound, potentially leading to the establishment of a new phonetic category for it. The SLM-r recognises that the L1 and L2 phonetic categories of a learner remain malleable across the lifespan in response to phonetic input, yet it envisages an 'end state' for those learners who are no longer exposed to phonetic input that differs from what they were exposed to earlier. By the same token, in the PAM-L2 perceptual discrimination is assumed to improve with new category acquisition through exposure to input that preserves phonetic differences. The underlying idea of a linear and incremental process of phonological development is, although not explicitly stated, reflected in terminology such as 'initial stage of learning' (Tyler, 2019, p. 619) and 'learning trajectory' (Tyler, 2019, p. 621).

Not only theoretical models but also much research in L2 phonological acquisition so far has foregrounded the conceptualisation of the language acquisition process as being incremental and overall linear. This means that development is typically modelled as a progression from one developmental point to another. In longitudinal research designs of this type, conclusions about language development are usually drawn based on differences between group averages at two or more points in time, while in cross-sectional research designs learners at different 'stages' or different levels of competence are measured once each and a development is inferred from the observed differences in their group means. For example, researchers interested in the discrimination of a phonetic contrast by a group of learners might collect data upon arrival in the target language country and two years later and then present the mean perception accuracy of the group at both data points. Alternatively, data from two learner groups, for example beginners and intermediate learners of a language, is collected at one point in time and the results are presented in the form of the mean scores of each group, with the beginners' score placed on the left and the intermediate learners' score on the right. Both these data collection methods and the interpretation of the results would suggest that language development is a linear process.

Thus, most research in the field of L2 acquisition so far is characterised by what Lowie (2017) refers to as 'product-orientation'. Product-oriented research focusses on the investigation of differences in language competence between groups of learners at one or more points in time. In a typical product-oriented study, one or more features of a learner's linguistic repertoire are measured at one or a few points in time and results are usually presented in the form of average group scores. Thus, the effect of specific factors such as different types of instruction can be determined by comparing, for example, the pronunciation accuracy of two learner groups before and after two types of pronunciation training. If one group has significantly higher scores after the training, one can conclude that their type of instruction is more effective.

Drawing conclusions about the language learning process based on group comparisons suggests that individual learners share a more or less uniform developmental process. In cross-sectional research designs, for example, the measurements obtained for particular learner groups such as beginners and intermediate learners are usually taken as representative for all learners at these stages. Thus, the developmental trends that are found by analysing specific learners or learner groups are often generalised to other learners and their language development. The observed variability between learners tends to be disregarded and is typically treated as 'noise' that needs to be ignored as it distorts the underlying general trends or effects. Accordingly, the traditional statistical methods employed to analyse such data, such as multivariate analyses and *t*-tests, often require a normal distribution and equal variances within groups. Nowadays, in order to account for learner variability, new statistical methods, such as mixed effect models, are employed for data analyses.

In recent years, questions have been raised about these implicit assumptions on language development which are reflected in theoretical models and 'traditional' empirical research alike, i.e., product-orientation, the modelling of the developmental process as an overall linear progression and the assumption that learners share a relatively uniform process of language development (e.g., de Bot & Larsen-Freeman, 2011; de Bot et al., 2007). In particular, there is a growing interest in aspects of language development that have been less in focus in the traditional research approaches – for example, the investigation of developmental processes rather than learner competence at different stages of language acquisition or a focus on individual learners and their variability rather than on general or universal trends that are assumed to apply across all learners. This new perspective is also evidenced in the recently revised SLM-r (Flege & Bohn, 2021), outlined in Section 2. The model now directs its focus on individual learner performance over time and the reorganisation of a learner's phonological system in response to dynamic changes in phonetic input.

Hammarberg (2017) describes these two approaches to investigating language development as differing in their perspective and timescale. He refers to the 'traditional' line of research with its focus on learner competence, the development of the learners' linguistic repertoire over time and the (universal) stages and sequences of learning as having a macro perspective, while the 'new' approach focusses on the micro level. Research on the micro level concentrates on specific situations of language use by a learner as well as the conditions and factors that influence their language use in such situations, for example their pronunciation of words when reading out a word list several times. It is assumed that in every situation where language is used, language elements or skills might be learned, which in turn contribute to the learner's language development over time. Hammarberg does not present the two approaches as exclusive but rather as complementary and connected. He argues that it is the individual events of language use that form the basis for evolving patterns and changes in the linguistic repertoire. In other words, a learner's language system develops from repeated language use in specific situations, with the recurrent activation of linguistic elements leading to their cognitive entrenchment, i.e., their being stored in the speaker's memory Thus, the more a specific word, phrase or pronunciation is being used, the likelier it is to be remembered and used again. Languages are thus pictured as adaptable systems that emerge from the learner's experiences in concrete events of language use.

3.2 The Complex Dynamic Systems Theory of Language Development

Complex Dynamic Systems Theory (CDST) is based on a model of the L2/L3 language learning process whose theoretical focus and applied methodologies differ from the traditional lines of research and their emphasis on linear conceptualisations of language acquisition and product-orientation as described in Section 3.1. In contrast to other models, CDST explicitly posits that language development is a non-linear, dynamic and self-organising process (Larsen-Freeman, 2009). The research focus does not lie on general trends based on group averages, but it zooms in on the developmental processes evidenced in individual learners that lead to those general trends. CDST assumes that all languages of a learner form part of one complex system that consists of several subsystems which are all interconnected (de Bot, 2012). In addition, while a system consists of several subsystems, it itself forms part of a larger system. For example, a speaker's language system consists of the phonological, the lexical and the syntactic subsystems while it forms part of the speaker's cognitive system. Relationships between subsystems can differ in their strength and can be supportive, competitive or conditional (Spoelman & Verspoor, 2010). In supportive relationships, one subsystem will contribute to the improvement of another; for example, the development of the pronunciation of one sound might support the accuracy of the pronunciation of another, and their development is typically synchronous. By contrast, in competitive relationships between subsystems, development is asynchronous and growth in one subsystem will result in the decline of another subsystem; for example, the perceptual accuracy of a sound contrast in one language might increase alongside a temporary decline in the perception of the same contrast in another language. A third option for a relationship between different subsystems is that one subsystem needs to be in place before another one can start developing, as proposed, for example, in some theorising about the relationship between segmental perception and production in L2 speech learning (Flege, 1995; Nagle, 2018).

Language development in the CDST framework is seen as dynamic, i.e., as a changing complex system over time. Changes can be caused by both internal and external forces, and changes in one subsystem always give rise to changes in the other subsystems. Thus, a learner's motivation to learn vocabulary, their language learning aptitude, the time spent on revision as well as their knowledge of other languages all can influence the learning of new words in a language, which in turn may affect the learner's ability to form more complex sentences in this language and boost the vocabulary learning of another language. Different types of change are presumed to occur: some are continuous, others discontinuous and often chaotic (van Dijk & van Geert, 2007). Due to the system's constant interaction with its environment as well as its internal changes, the system is observed to never stop changing. Rather, it will continually reorganise itself, changing its form from one relatively stable preferred state or 'attractor state' to another. In summary, in the CDST conceptualisation, language development is non-linear and unpredictable: in a complex system with numerous interacting subsystems, even the tiniest changes to one subsystem can cause the entire system to change. Changes in the different subsystems can occur slowly or 'in leaps and bounds' and they can conspire to move the entire system into a reorganisation process. However, there seem to be preferred states and directions for the system (de Bot & Larsen-Freeman, 2011, p. 15) such as a seeming stagnation of learning or general trends in language development. Moreover, due to the complex interaction of the numerous variables and subsystems, it is difficult if not impossible to predict the exact shape and direction in which the complex system will develop.

CDST stresses the crucial effect of the initial conditions, which may have far-reaching effects on the processes of change of the system (de Bot & Larsen-Freeman, 2011, p.10). This consideration is clearly most relevant for the context of learning a new L3, where the initial condition will entail knowledge of both the L1 and the L2. CDST does not, however, assume an endpoint of language development and therefore avoids the term 'acquisition' that implies this. In the CDST framework, it is acknowledged that linguistic skills can always grow and decline and that learners undergo continuous developmental processes. Thus, even the language system of a highly advanced learner and the first language of a speaker are not assumed to remain stable but they are likely to undergo changes due to external forces and the interaction of their subsystems.

Furthermore, in the CDST approach to language development, inter- and intra-learner variability is treated as meaningful rather than an issue to be controlled for in order to find significant differences between conditions (de Bot et al., 2007; Lowie, 2011). It is considered essential for a description of the process of language development and a sign of self-organisation of the language system. Variability across learners (inter-speaker variability) occurs due to their different initial conditions such as prior linguistic knowledge, and cognitive and affective factors as well as the different influences of external and internal variables, making it impossible to generalise from the language learning process of one learner to the processes of others. In the CDST approach, intra-speaker variability is seen as a driving force of development and as an indicator for ongoing developmental processes (Spoelman & Verspoor, 2010). It is assumed that the degree of intra-speaker variability can help to explain how the language system of a learner changes over time: low intra-speaker variability (e.g., highly consistent pronunciation of a word across multiple occasions) is taken to indicate that the speaker's language system is relatively stable and settled into an attractor state, while a high degree of variability is interpreted as an indication that developmental changes are currently taking place. If two distinct variability patterns or variability ranges can be identified in the individual's learning trajectory, commonly marked by an unexpectedly large peak or spike at the moment of the transition, the learner's language system is understood to have moved into a different level of development (van Dijk & van Geert, 2007; Larsen-Freeman & Cameron, 2008). The CDST approach is interested in identifying and describing the transformative transition between such phases to appreciate the different shapes a developmental change can take.

In summary, CDST and the traditional linear model of language 'acquisition' differ in their focus in the following ways. In CDST,

- language development is not presumed to be linear over time but is conceptualised as non-linear and dynamic: it is characterised by increasing and decreasing variability as well as subsequent phases of relative stability
- language development is seen to be constantly changing without reaching a stable end point

- language development is not presumed to be similar across language learners and thus the research focus lies on describing individual learning processes
- not all variability in the learning process can be explained by external influences because some variability is an intrinsic property of a self-organising, dynamic system
- only the fact that changes will happen in the system can be predicted but not the exact outcomes of these changes; thus, an individual learner cannot be seen as a generalisable hypothetical representative of a larger learner population.

3.3 New Methods of Studying Language Development

The underlying theoretical assumptions and research goals of CDST mean that studies carried out within this framework require a whole set of new research methods. They present challenges to and cannot be answered by using the traditional methods. For example, researchers in the CDST framework do not search for simple linear causal relationships, such as the influence of two different types of input on the perception of a particular sound, because they assume that there are many contributing variables to the development of speech perception, such as other languages known, the quality of the phonological working memory or exposure to orthographic representations of the sound, which might in turn influence each other and which are not stable but change over time. Rather than focussing on individual variables, researchers in the CDST framework focus on patterns of co-variability and try to analyse as many subsystems as possible including their interactions. They study patterns of variability over time by charting the dynamic interaction of related subsystems (e.g., Verspoor et al., 2011; Lowie, 2017). Studies in the CDST framework thus typically employ what has been called a process-oriented method: the research design is longitudinal involving learner groups or individuals from whom data is collected at numerous densely spaced data points and the analyses focus on the description of the dynamic changes in L2/L3 development.

Hammarberg's (2017) small-scale study on Swedish word production by L1 German learners exemplifies this method. The participants were shown cards by a test leader who pronounced them once and were asked to name the objects themselves. The set of cards was presented three times during each of three sessions: immediately after arriving in Sweden, one month and two months later. The experiment thus yielded learner pronunciations multiple times and on three different timescales: the immediate repetitions after having been shown a card, the three repetitions of a word within one session and the repetitions across the different testing sessions. This method allowed the author to detect the learners' variable productions within each session and over time, the points in time when productions settled into an 'attractor state' reflected by invariable pronunciations as well as differences across learners in terms of both variability and the point when the attractor state was reached.

Similarly, Yu and Lowie (2019) adopted a dense data collection procedure and recorded the oral English performance of Chinese learners of English ten times in weekly intervals over ten weeks. They showed that while at the group level the learners improved both their lexical and syntactic complexity as well as accuracy in oral English, individual learners showed unique patterns of development which were argued to be influenced by the initial condition of their learning path.

Working within a CDST framework not only requires different methods in terms of data collection but also necessitates the use of different statistical methods that are able to detect and compare the learners' individual developments on different timescales as well as major shifts in their language system. Studies based on the assumption of a linear developmental process and aiming at discovering general trends usually employ mean scores and standard deviations and imply the normal distribution of their data in the search of discovering the effects of individual factors on the linguistic competence of learners and the developmental process. By contrast, the research design of CDST-inspired studies yields longitudinal individual data collected at dense intervals in order to reveal any changes in language development. (For a detailed overview of such methods, see Verspoor et al., 2011)

The moving min-max graph, for example, is a descriptive data analysis technique that visualises a learner's dynamic developmental process and highlights the intra-learner variability while keeping the raw data visible (van Dijk et al., 2011). This method uses a fixed window, a time frame comprising, for example, five data points that continuously moves ahead one data point. Each consecutive window thus largely overlaps with the preceding one, differing only in the first and last data point. For each of these windows, the maximum and minimum values are calculated, displaying the bandwidth of the observed scores. This method thus shows the amount of variation at each period of time in relation to sudden developmental 'jumps' that might reflect the internal reorganisation of the language system (van Dijk et al., 2011, p. 76).

Moreover, a moving correlation can be calculated to estimate the relationship between two language subsystems. For this, like for the moving min-max technique, a time window is defined and the correlation coefficient is calculated between two data sets for all points within this window. The window is then moved along the data set by the next data point and the correlation coefficient is calculated at every fixed time window. This technique shows whether developments of different features in a language system are synchronous or not and allows the characterisation of such relationships as competitive or supportive.

Resampling techniques can be employed for testing the significance of fluctuations in variability. This method 'consists of randomly drawing a large number of subsamples ... from the original sample' (van Dijk et al., 2011, p. 77). After defining the variable that serves as the testing criterion, a resampling model is set up and the original data is randomly reshuffled a predefined number of times (e.g., 7,000 times). The original data set is then compared to each of these resampled data sets, testing the observations against chance. This Monte Carlo analysis thus calculates, for example, how often a peak similar to the one found in the data set occurs when the data is shuffled randomly. Yu and Lowie (2019) considered a peak significant when it occurred fewer than 250 times in 10,000 rounds of reshuffling.

An alternative technique of modelling language development at a group level is Generalised Additive Mixed Modelling (GAMM). The method uses smooth terms to account for time-varying patterns in individual data, it provides the option of including nonlinear interactions with two or more numeric predictors and it can tackle the issue of temporal autocorrelation. As such, it seems particularly useful for exploring fluctuations, trends and interactions as well as intra-individual variation in time-series data (Pfenninger, 2021).

3.4 Motivation for the Present Study on Multilingual Phonological Development

A large number of studies on language development carried out within the CDST framework have yielded important insights such as:

- Learning trends observed in learner group comparisons most often do not reflect the learning processes of individual learners (van Dijk et al., 2011).
- The language development of individuals can be very diverse, even for identical twins learning a language in similar settings (Chan et al., 2015).
- Variability is an inherent property of language development and can sometimes serve as its driving force (e.g., Dong, 2016; Penris & Verspoor, 2017; Verspoor et al., 2011).
- The interaction between several language subsystems can be supportive, competitive or conditional and may change over time (e.g., Spoelman & Verspoor, 2010).

However, so far CDST-based studies have focussed almost exclusively on linguistic levels other than phonology (but see theoretical and pedagogical contributions by Lima Jr., 2013; Lima Jr. & Alves, 2019) and, for the most part, do not specifically investigate the entire language system of the learners but analyse only their target language (cf. Lowie, 2011). Typically, longitudinal data is collected at close intervals in order to trace the variability in performance as well as overall developmental trends in the learners' target language while ignoring their L1 and further foreign languages. Thus, it has so far been rarely tested whether the relationships found to operate between a learner's different linguistic subsystems also apply to their different languages (for an exception, see Huang et al., 2020). It is therefore the aim of this Element to present one of the first studies on phonetic and phonological development by multilingual speakers within the framework of CDST that seeks to contribute to this theory. In particular, we would like to show which insights using longitudinal, individual and dense data can contribute to describing and understanding phonetic and phonological development and how this approach can complement traditional product-oriented research designs.

In other words, it is the object of this study to test whether the findings that were obtained in the studies concentrating on other linguistic levels that were discussed in this section also apply to phonetics and phonology. Specifically, the following hypotheses will be tested:

1. Learning trends in phonetic and phonological development that are observed through learner group comparisons do not model well the learning processes of individual learners (cf. van Dijk et al., 2011).
2. Learners' variability at the micro level influences and correlates with their long-term phonetic and phonological development (cf. Hammarberg, 2017).
3. Extreme variability at one point in time signals (upcoming) major developmental changes (van Dijk & van Geert, 2007; Evans & Larsen-Freeman, 2020).
4. Different phonetic and phonological features develop in interaction with each other (cf. Yu & Lowie, 2019).
5. The perception and production of speech sounds co-evolve (Flege & Bohn, 2021).
6. The developmental relationship between a learner's foreign languages is initially competitive and subsequently supportive, and it changes with proficiency (cf. Yu & Lowie, 2019; Huang et al., 2020).

4 Study: Multilingual Development of Phonetics and Phonology

4.1 Method

4.1.1 Design

A longitudinal study design was implemented to shed light on intra- and inter-individual processes of the phonetic and phonological development of multilingual speakers. A group of sixteen learners with a similar language profile

(L1 German, L2 English, L3 Polish) was recorded in all of their languages four times (T1–T4) within the first year of L3 learning. In addition, in between T2 and T4, a small subset of these participants consisting of three learners recorded themselves at home in their L2 and L3 every week for eighteen weeks (dense data collection; DDC). All testing sessions were designed to elicit certain phonetic and phonological features which were either shared by the languages or not (see Section 4.1.4). This way, potential interactions between the language subsystems over time can be revealed.

Figure 1 visualises the longitudinal data collection with four main group testing times. It commenced a month after the start of L3 Polish lessons and stretched over the first ten months of L3 learning (T1 at five weeks, T2 at ten weeks, T3 at five months and T4 at ten months into L3 learning). Due to the expectation that there would be less development in the learners' L1 than in their non-native languages, L1 production data was collected at T1 and T4 only, along with other background measures such as the learners' language attitudes and cross-linguistic phonological awareness. In their L2 and L3, the participants completed various production and perception tasks (see Section 4.1.3) at all four group testing times. Between the third and seventh month of L3 learning, three adults each participated in eighteen weekly dense testing sessions for which

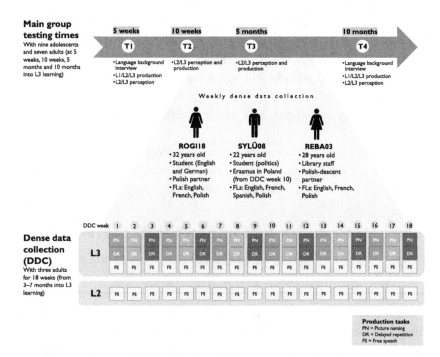

Figure 1 Visualisation of data collection timeline.

they recorded themselves at home in their L2 and L3. Each week they also provided information on their language learning activity and progress that week. The general language learning profile of these three as well as the other participants are described in the following section.

4.1.2 Participants

In total, sixteen beginner learners of L3 Polish took part in the longitudinal study. Nine of them were adolescents of the same age group (12–13 years; 5 females, 4 males), and the remaining seven adults were between 21 and 39 years old (5 females, 2 males). All of them shared German as L1 and English as L2, the latter of which they had learned or were still learning in school within their L1 environment (Germany). In addition, five of the adults also had some knowledge of French and/or Spanish, which they had acquired in secondary school. Although they were tested in these additional languages as well, only English and Polish are the focus of this enquiry, as these are the foreign languages the participants were actively using at the time this study was conducted. The two age groups were matched regarding their L3 Polish input, which amounted to three hours per week. For all participants, Polish was a completely new language, i.e., all heritage speakers were excluded from the final data set, as were all early bilinguals.

The adult participants, aged 21–39 (mean age = 26.4), were recruited from community college and university language classes and received a small financial compensation for participating in the study. They had started learning their L2 English in a formal context (at primary or secondary school) at a mean age of 9.4 years and self-assessed their language skills as upper-intermediate to advanced.

Three out of the seven adults participated in the DDC, recording themselves at home in their L2 and L3 every week for eighteen weeks (see Figure 1). The two females, REBA03 (aged 28) and ROGI18 (aged 32), decided to take Polish classes with the aim to be able to better communicate with their partners' Polish families (they both spoke German to their Polish partners). REBA03 was a university librarian, and ROGI18 was in the second year of studying to become a secondary school teacher of English and German. The male participant, SYLÜ08 (aged 22), was a politics student who took Polish classes before going to Poland for four months as part of an Erasmus exchange. He was still in Germany at T1 and T2 of the group testing times and the first nine weeks of the DDC. From DDC week 10, he recorded himself from Poland. The final group testing time (T4) took place shortly after his return to Germany. These three participants were chosen for the dense data collection because they had demonstrated at T1 a number of non-target-like pronunciations in both their L2 and L3, which made changes in their phonological system more likely than for the other participants who showed mainly target-like pronunciations in their L2 or L3 or both. Shifts in the phonological system were expected especially for SYLÜ08, given the changes in the language learning environment in the course of the study.

The younger L3 learners, aged 12–13, were recruited at a school located in Germany within close proximity to the Polish border. They all chose Polish as a new subject (over French) and were total beginners as well. All of them had been receiving instruction in their L2 English for several years, their mean age of onset of L2 learning being younger than those of the adults at 6.5 years. The difference of the two groups' starting age has to do with educational policies in Germany that had changed over the years regarding the school year in which English is introduced as a mandatory subject. Alongside their Polish lessons, the adolescents also had four 45-minute English lessons at school (a total of three hours per week) throughout the time span of the research project. They self-assessed their L2 skills as lower-intermediate.

4.1.3 Data Collection

The data collection comprised a language background interview, three different production tasks and two perception tasks. For each language (L1 German, L2 English and L3 Polish), the tasks were administered on different days and by a research assistant who addressed the participants in the target language only. The research assistants were native speakers of German and Polish respectively and native or near-native speakers of English.

Language background interview. An extensive language background inter-view was conducted as part of the L1 recording sessions at both main testing times (T1 and T4). This structured interview covered many aspects considered potentially important with regard to the participants' language development such as their language learning history, language use and attitudes.

Production task 1: Delayed repetition (DR). In this task, the participants heard a stimulus word in a carrier phrase in the L1, L2 and L3 ('Ich sage X zu dir' in German, 'I say X to you/again' in English and 'Mówię X do ciebie' in Polish). After a prompt (e.g., 'And what do you say?' in English) spoken by a different speaker, the learners repeated the entire first phrase (with the inter-stimulus interval set at 1,000 ms). The delayed repetition task was selected as it effectively elicits speech production even in low-proficiency speakers and reduces the risk of direct imitation by including a distractor phrase. The stimuli were presented in two randomised orders and embedded in a PowerPoint presentation as a self-paced task. The testing block was preceded by a practice block of three trial items.

Production task 2: Picture naming (PN). In this task, the participants were presented with a series of simple pictures in a PowerPoint presentation (one picture per slide). They were selected from a range of categories that language learners are typically exposed to in the earlier stages of language learning such as colours, animals and foods. Concerning the L3 stimuli, the respective Polish teachers had been consulted to assure that the vocabulary items had been covered in class. This task was self-paced.

Production task 3: Storytelling (ST). The participants were given a different eight-frame picture story for each language to elicit free speech. They were granted as much time as they needed to familiarise themselves with the pictures and the simple storyline before they were asked to tell it. The picture stories contained a number of objects and actions suitable to elicit the items of interest, and the research assistant administering the task made sure to guide and prompt the participant to name some of them after the participants' first rendition if necessary.

Perception task 1: Forced-choice goodness (FC). In the forced-choice goodness task, the participants heard two renditions of the same phrase differing only on the stimulus items embedded in a carrier phase and had to decide which one sounded more natural. One rendition was a target realisation and the other was an accented language realisation in which only the target sound was manipulated, i.e., realised as the L1, L2 or L3 sound respectively. For example, in the L2 English version of the task, the rhotic stimuli included the target-like phrase 'You will hear the word ring [ɹɪŋ]' followed by the Polish-like realisation of the rhotic sound 'You will hear the word ring [rɪŋ]', as well as stimuli including pairs of English and German-like rhotics. In the L3 Polish session, the stimuli included Polish target rhotics as well as German and English rhotics. The carrier sentences were always consistent with the language of the session.

The stimuli were recorded by female native speakers of the respective languages who were fluent advanced speakers of the other two languages in the triad of languages. The stimuli were randomised and counterbalanced across trials in E-Prime 2.0 (Psychology Software Tools, Pittsburgh, PA). The testing block was preceded by three trial items. The inter-stimulus interval was set at 500 ms and the participants had a 3,000 ms response limit. The response accuracy and reaction time were recorded.

Perception task 2: ABX. While the forced-choice task was administered to test the learners' judgement of naturalness employing cross-language sound contrasts, ABX tasks test language-specific contrasts (Strange & Shafer, 2008). Such timed discrimination tasks assess the learners' ability to distinguish between two minimally contrasting sounds within a language, as for example /v/ and /w/ in English and Polish. Therefore, this perception task was adopted for testing the phonemic contrast between /v/ and /w/ but not the allophonic contrasts of the other three features investigated in the study. In the ABX task, the participants listened to a pair of stimuli (AB) recorded by one speaker. Subsequently, they heard a third stimulus (X) produced by a different speaker which was either the same as the first (A) or the second one (B). The participants then had to decide whether the final stimulus (X) was more like the first (A) or the second one (B) by pressing a button on a button box (see Figure 2 for a visualisation of the task procedure). The trials were randomised so that the minimal pairs included appeared in all possible combinations (ABA, ABB, BAB, BAA). Like in the case of the FC task, the ABX task was administered through E-Prime 2.0 measuring accuracy and response times. If no response was logged within 3,000 ms after the last stimulus, the trial was coded as incorrect, and the experiment automatically proceeded with the next trial.

Production tasks dense data collection. The weekly dense data collection included a picture naming, a delayed repetition and a different free speech production task in the L3 every week, with the free speech tasks having been carefully compiled in line with current topics and vocabulary from the participants' L3 classes. For the L2 session, the free speech element was the only task since the learners were much more fluent in English and were expected to

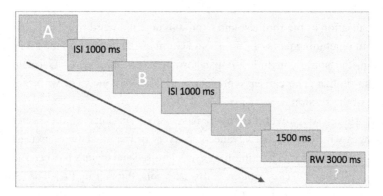

Figure 2 ABX task procedure (adapted from Nelson, 2020; p. 38). ISI = inter-stimulus interval, RW = response window.

produce sufficient tokens of interest in this single task. To help the participants to tune into the appropriate language mode, the free speech prompt was a short video recording featuring the L2 research assistant (who also collected the L2 data at the group testing times, so they were familiar with the person and already associated them with English). In the video, the research assistant briefly talked about a specific topic and then asked an open-ended question related to that topic which the participants were asked to respond to or talk about for about one minute. Perception dense data in the L2 and L3 was also obtained, but it is not included in our analyses here.

4.2 Features under Investigation

Four phonetic and phonological features were chosen as the focus of this study, all of which differ between the three languages to some extent. Table 1 offers an overview of the production and perception tasks used to elicit them along with a description of how they are typically realised in the three languages. Each of the features (and the measures applied in their analysis) is described in greater detail in the following section, including predictions of learnability for the study partici-pants, based on the L2 models presented in Section 2. These are to be rendered with care, however, as the predictions for discrimination difficulty of sound contrasts (PAM/PAM-L2), for the perception and production of sound segments (SLM/ SLM-r), and for the production of sound segments and universal phono-logical processes (OPM) were put forth for L2 rather than for L3 speech learning scenarios in the models, i.e., without considering a possibility of an interaction between the target language sound system and that of other foreign languages. The acoustic measurements were completed by three phonetically trained raters in Praat (Boersma & Weenink, 2021). Whenever the second rater did not agree with the transcription of the first one, the third rater decided between the two.

4.2.1 /v-w/ Contrast

Previous studies have shown that the contrast between the voiced labiodental fricative /v/ and the labiovelar approximant /w/, as it exists in English and Polish, can be challenging for L1 speakers of German in both perception (Iverson et al., 2008; Ankerstein & Morschett, 2013) and production (Pascoe, 1987). This is partly because /w/ does not exist in the German sound inventory but also because /v/ is typically produced slightly differently in German than it is in English and Polish. In German, /v/ is commonly realised as a weak labiodental approximant [ʋ] and is therefore phonetically speaking almost in between English and Polish /w/ and /v/. Within the pair, and in correspondence with the predictions of the SLM/SLM-r (Flege, 1995; Flege & Bohn, 2021), English /v/ may be the

Table 1 Overview of features, tasks, and typical realisation in each of the languages.

Feature	Tasks (production; perception)	Realisation in German (L1)	Realisation in (British) English (L2)	Realisation in Polish (L3)
/v-w/ contrast	DR, PN, ST; ABX	only /v/ exists	both /v/ and /w/ exist (but higher frequency of /w/ than /v/)	both /v/ and /w/ exist (but higher frequency of /v/ than /w/)
Final obstruents (de)voicing	DR, PN, ST; FC	always devoices final obstruents	typically maintains a distinction between voiced and voiceless final obstruents	usually devoices final obstruents
Vowel reduction	DR, PN, ST; FC	some degree of vowel reduction in unstressed syllables	clear reduction of nearly every unstressed syllable	no vowel reduction
Rhotics	DR, PN, ST; FC	voiced uvular fricative /ʁ/; sometimes voiced uvular trill [ʀ]	voiced postalveolar approximant /ɹ/	voiced alveolar trill /r/; sometimes tap [ɾ] (the latter especially in fast speech)

more challenging member to learn to produce by L1 German speakers, as it is the more similar sound to German /v/ than English /w/ is (Iverson et al., 2008). If this distinction is made perceptually by L1 German learners, the PAM/PAM-L2 (Best, 1995; Best & Tyler, 2007) would predict a moderate discrimination accuracy for such a category-goodness type of a sound contrast.

4.2.2 Final Obstruent (De)voicing

The languages in the learners' repertoire also differ in their realisation of coda obstruents such as /b/, /d/, /g/ and /v/. While English retains a voicing contrast in syllable-final positions (e.g., between *bad* vs. *bat*), final obstruents are always devoiced in German and most of the time in Polish (Rubach, 1984; Smith et al., 2007). Many L2 studies have reported learning difficulties of the phonological process of syllable-final voicing by speakers of different L1 backgrounds (e.g., Cebrian, 2000; Dmitrieva et al., 2010), accounting for their results by the marked-ness status of final obstruent voicing. This theorising is in line with such production-based L2 speech learning models as the OPM (Major, 2001). The same outcome would be predicted by the SLM/SLM-r (Flege, 1995; Flege & Bohn, 2021) for L1 German speakers perceiving and producing L2 English word-final obstruents, albeit on the account of their use of L1-based cue-weighting regarding vowel duration and/or closure voicing rather than due to the markedness of the phonological process. In terms of L3 Polish final obstruent devoicing, L1 German speakers would thus be predicted in the model to be facilitated in the learning of devoiced word-final obstruents. The PAM/PAM-L2 (Best, 1995; Best & Tyler, 2007) focusses on the perception of sound contrasts and does not make any predictions about phonological processes.

4.2.3 Vowel Reduction

The learners' languages German and English both clearly differentiate between stressed and unstressed syllables by making a difference in vowel duration in combination with other characteristics (different vowel quality, increased pitch and increased intensity). The languages differ, however, in the extent to which unstressed vowels are reduced, with English being more extreme in that regard. Therefore, as would be predicted in the SLM/SLM-r (Flege, 1995; Flege & Bohn, 2021) for highly similar features, numerous studies have reported vowel reduction as challenging for L2 learners of English with L1 German and vice versa (e.g., Gut, 2010). In Polish, on the other hand, vowels in unstressed syllables are not reduced, resulting in a similar duration and quality for vowels in stressed and unstressed positions. As the existing theoretical models of L2 speech learning focus on sound segments, they cannot be straightforwardly applied to other aspects of L2 speech such as phonological processes or prosody and its various properties. A study on unstressed vowel reduction in L3 Brazilian Portuguese by Ribeiro (2021) suggests, however, that this prosodic feature may show a combined cross-linguistic influence in learners who have experience with both reducing and non-reducing languages.

4.2.4 Rhotics

Rhotics are realised distinctly in the three languages of the learners in this study. Standard German mainly uses voiced uvular fricatives /ʁ/ as well as some uvular trills [ʀ] (Kohler, 1999). In most varieties of English, rhotics are realised as a postalveolar approximant /ɹ/ or a retroflex approximant [ɻ], which can sometimes be labialised to [ɹʷ] (Roach, 2004). Polish has both voiced alveolar trills /r/ and taps [ɾ] as free-variant allophones, the latter of which is primarily used intervocalically and in fast speech (Jassem, 2003). Thus, according to the SLM/SLM-r (Flege, 1995; Flege & Bohn, 2021), the new L2 and L3 rhotic sounds should be relatively easy to learn for L1 German speakers, at least in terms of perceptual discrimination, although alveolar trills, in particular, can be articulatorily challenging sounds to acquire (Catford, 2001). The PAM/PAM-L2 (Best, 1995; Best & Tyler, 2007) does not make any predictions for the perception of individual sounds but rather focusses on sound contrasts only.

4.3 Data Analysis

Following previous L3 studies in the field (e.g., Kopečková et al., 2016; Cabrelli, 2016; Nelson, 2022), inferential statistics were eschewed in favour of descriptive statistics for most of the individual data as well as group analyses. Plonsky (2015, p. 30), for instance, calls for the implementation of descriptive statistics when power is low due to small sample sizes, which is the case here. Moreover, as stated in the Introduction, this study aims to describe the process of language development and its dynamic changes, which many inferential methods are not geared towards. The exact coding and analysis process applied for each feature is described in what follows.

4.3.1 /v-w/ Contrast

The learners' ability to distinguish between the two sounds perceptually, tested in the ABX task ($n = 24$ for L2 and $n = 24$ for L3), was calculated as a per cent accuracy score for each learner and testing time. For the three production tasks, the sounds ($n = 14$ for L1, $n = 24$ for L2 and $n = 14$ for L3) were auditorily analysed, transcribed and coded for accuracy by the three phonetically trained raters. Due to the nature of the free speech task and because not all tokens were produced in the picture naming task, some learners produced more or fewer tokens in total. The report of the production results is limited to /w/ in the study, as this member of the contrast was expected to be more likely to show developmental changes in the multilinguals' production (cf. Iverson et al., 2008).

4.3.2 Final Obstruent (De)voicing

The perception of final voiced and devoiced obstruents, tested in the FC task ($n = 13$ for L2 and $n = 16$ for L3), was analysed in terms of accuracy percentage for each multilingual learner at each testing time. For the production of (underlying) voiced final obstruents ($n = 16$ for L1, $n = 17$ for L2 and $n = 16$ for L3), as tested in the three production tasks, three measures were analysed, mirroring the method of previous studies on final obstruent (de)voicing (e.g., Smith et al., 2007; Smith & Peterson, 2012):

- duration of the vowel preceding the final voiced obstruent in ms,
- duration of the closure portion of the final voiced obstruent in ms, and
- duration of the release portion or burst of the final voiced obstruent in ms.

The segmentation was done according to commonly utilised acoustic characteristics associated with substantial changes in waveform shape and/or amplitude and spectrographic events. The end of the vowel was set at the drop in amplitude in the waveform following Smith et al. (2007) and Smith and Peterson (2012). The duration of the release portion was measured from the onset of sudden discontinuity in the waveform and spectrogram until the end of the visible noise in the spectrogram. In addition, it was transcribed whether the obstruent was followed by a new word beginning with a voiced or voiceless sound or by a pause. This is relevant especially for the target production of Polish word-final obstruents, which are voiced when followed by a voiced sound (undergoing regressive assimilation of voicing; a process that does not occur in German). All three duration parameters were submitted to phase-shift analyses of the weekly dense data collected from three adult multilinguals, in order to detect any major developmental changes in their realisation of (underlying) voiced final obstruents. To this end, use was made of the Change-Point Analyzer Software (Version 2.3; Taylor, 2021), which combines cumulative sum charts and bootstrap methods to detect statistically significant changes in time-series data and calculates a confidence interval of any changes for the data points.

4.3.3 Vowel Reduction

The participants' perception of naturalness of vowel reduction, tested in the FC task ($n = 5$ for L2 and $n = 4$ for L3), was calculated as an accuracy score for each learner and testing time. In the three production tasks ($n = 17$ for L1, $n = 17$ for L2 and $n = 12$ for L3), the ratio of vowel length in stressed versus unstressed syllables was established. The duration of monophthongs (in ms) in stressed and unstressed syllables of all correctly stressed words was marked using the onset and offset of vowel formants as cues. The ratio was yielded by dividing the duration of an unstressed vowel by the duration of the immediately preceding stressed vowel within the same word (values of around 1 indicating same length of stressed and unstressed vowels, values below 1 indicating reduction of unstressed vowels, and values above 1 indicating longer duration of unstressed vowels). Moreover, it was annotated for each word whether it was phrase-final or not, as unstressed vowels in phrase-final words may be longer than those in non-final position within intonation phrases. Both average production accuracy at each main testing time and change point analyses of the weekly dense data were computed for this feature.

4.3.4 Rhotics

The learners' perception of naturalness of the different rhotics in L2 and L3, tested in the FC task ($n = 10$ for L2 and $n = 10$ for L3), was calculated as an accuracy score for each learner and testing time. The production data ($n = 10$ for L1, $n = 14$ for L2 and $n = 10$ for L3) that was collected in the three tasks was analysed auditorily, transcribing all instances of the learners' rhotic sound realisations using a range of IPA symbols, and analysed for accuracy. The rate of the production accuracy was calculated in raw numbers as well as percentages for each learner.

5 Results

First, we present an overview of the whole data set for perception and production results separately. Figure 3 displays the perception accuracy of the /v-w/ contrast, the rhotics, final voiced obstruents and vowel reduction by the sixteen learners in both their L2 English and their L3 Polish at T1, T2, T3 and T4 (for the features rhotics, final voiced obstruents and vowel reduction no data was collected in L3 Polish at T1). Only the perception of the /v-w/ contrast was elicited via an ABX task, while the perception of the remaining features was elicited via an FC task. It shows that the perception accuracy varies across the phonological/phonetic features and processes with the perception of the rhotics having the highest and the perception of final voiced obstruents having the lowest accuracy overall. Only for the perception of /r/ in L3 Polish and the perception of final voiced obstruents in both L2 and L3 can differences between the adolescents and the adult learners be observed. Overall, perception accuracy of a particular phonological feature or process is very similar in both the learners' L2 and the L3. Variation across the individual speakers, however, is

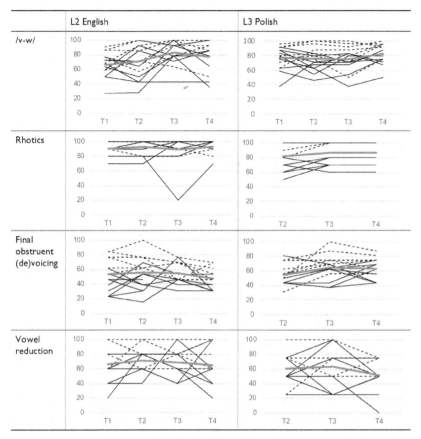

Figure 3 Mean accuracy of perception of /v-w/, the rhotics, final (underlying) voiced obstruents and vowel reduction by the sixteen learners in their L2 English and their L3 Polish at T1, T2, T3 and T4 (at T1 in L3 Polish only for /v-w/). Adult learners are represented by dotted lines. The group mean values are indicated by the bold line.

evident for all features except the rhotics, where perception accuracy is above 60 per cent in their L2 English for all learners.

Figure 4 shows the mean values of accurate production of /w/, the rhotics and vowel reduction (= the mean vowel ratio) by the sixteen learners in both their L2 English and L3 Polish at T1, T2, T3 and T4 (only T2 and T4 for vowel reduction). The production results for final voiced obstruents are not reported at this point as this feature was analysed in the study in terms of three different duration parameters rather than an accuracy score. Both /w/ and the rhotics show distinct patterns from each other but appear similar across both languages and both age groups: while /w/ is produced fairly accurately in L2 English and L3 Polish by most adolescents and

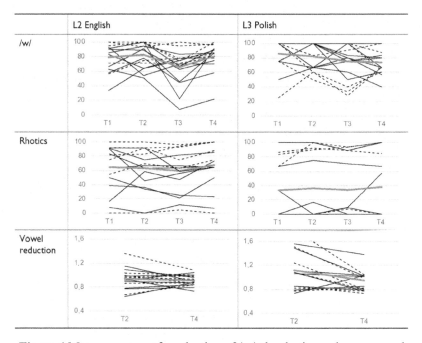

Figure 4 Mean accuracy of production of /w/, the rhotics and mean vowel duration ratio by the learners in their L2 English and L3 Polish. Values of around 1.0 for mean vowel duration ratio indicate the same length of stressed and unstressed vowels. Adult learners are represented by dotted lines. The group mean values are indicated by the bold line.

adults, the accuracy of the rhotics is much more diverse with individual learners at ceiling level in both languages and others not producing them accurately at all. The two age groups were also comparable in their production of vowel reduction in that they showed some progress, in a target-like direction, with less reduced forms in their L3 Polish than in their L2 English, as suggested by the score for mean vowel duration ratio around 1.0 for L3 Polish. A high degree of inter-learner variability was nevertheless also evident in the L3 Polish.

Here, the results for each of our hypotheses (see Section 3.4) are presented.

H1. Learning trends in phonetic and phonological development that are observed through learner group comparisons do not model well the learning processes of individual learners

Figures 3 and 4 show that the group average values depicted in bold do not model well the learning processes of the individual learners. In fact, not a single one of the sixteen learners shows a development that matches the group mean value in any of the phonetic or phonological features or two languages.

H2. Learners' variability at the micro level influences and correlates with their long-term phonetic and phonological development.

Figure 5 displays the sixteen learners' variability of producing the rhotics in their three languages at T1, T2 and T4. The variability was calculated by dividing the number of different sounds per token produced at one point in time, irrespective of them being target-like or not, and multiplied by 100. For example, BISC14 produced five words containing /r/ in Polish at T1 and realised the rhotic in three different ways: three times as the uvular trill [ʀ] and once each as the uvular fricative [ʁ] and the voiceless velar fricative [x]. Her calculated variability for L3 Polish at T1 is thus 3 (different realisations) / 5 (tokens) * 100 = 60.

Figure 5 shows clear differences across the multilinguals in terms of the variability of their realisations at the three data points T1, T2 and T4. DIMO03 and ROGI18 appear to be in a stable period of pronouncing the rhotic sound in their L2 English: they consistently realise it as the approximant [ɹ] during the ten months of our study but show some variation in their pronunciation of the rhotic in both their L1 and L3. While for DIMO03 this variation is entirely target-like in both L1 and L3 – for example, producing both the trill [r] and the

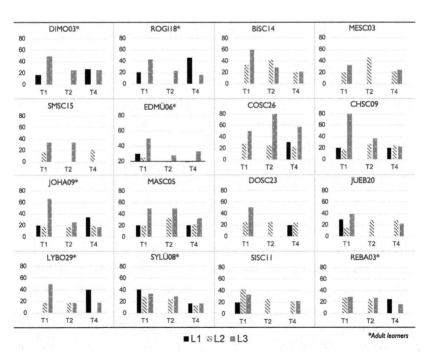

Figure 5 Variability of rhotic production for all learners in their three languages at T1, T2 and T4 (no L1 data is available for T2).

tap [ɾ] in Polish (see Table 1 in Section 4.2) – ROGI18's production of the Polish rhotic varies between [r], [ɾ] and non-target 'German' [ʁ]. Similarly, the three multilinguals BISC14, MESC03 and SMSC15 all demonstrate a non-variable realisation of the rhotic in their L1 German but exhibit some variability in the production of the rhotic in both L2 English and L3 Polish. Yet, while BISC14 produces non-target-like rhotics such as [ʁ] in both English and Polish at all data collection points and SMSC15 produces exclusively target-like rhotics in English only at T2 and never in Polish, MESC03 only produces some non-target-like rhotics in English at T2 and T4. For EDMÜ06, variability occurs in all three of his languages at T1 but is restricted to L3 Polish at T2 and T4. Thus, for five out of the sixteen multilinguals, production of the rhotic in one language is stable, which points towards an attractor state of this subsystem during the ten months of our study.

Another interesting observation concerns potential changes in some of the learners' L1. Six of the multilinguals produce the voiceless velar fricative [x] or a combined [ʁ/x] sound as the German rhotic at T4. In fact, half of the learners produced such sounds in their L3 Polish in the very early stages of learning to attempt the trill [r] when they were not able to produce it at all or not consistently. This non-acceptable realisation of rhotics in Polish, which is used in their L1 German at T4, can thus tentatively be interpreted as a special kind of L3-to-L1 influence, i.e., regressive CLI from an earlier production in the L3 to the L1 at a later stage of learning. This example highlights the complexity of cross-linguistic interaction, where an 'L1-coloured' sound from the learners' L3 repertoire can find its way back into their L1. Similarly, the production of uvular trills [ʀ] in German increases from T1 to T4. This can also be argued to be evidence for regressive CLI, as the learners produce more of the L1 variant with the L3-like manner of articulation. Hence, on this feature, these two languages seem to be more prone to mutual influence for some of the learners with their distinct yet articulatorily more similar rhotics than the English approximant [ɹ]. The L1 rhotic sounds (and other articulatorily similar L1 sounds) clearly seem to be the preferred basis for those struggling with the Polish tap or trill, which in turn also seems to make their L1 German more receptive to Polish-like sounds.

Figure 5 thus also shows highly individual relationships between variability at the micro level, i.e., single realisations at one particular data collection point, and long-term development at the macro level, i.e., a potentially stable state after ten months of learning. Of those multilinguals that show target-like pronunciation of the rhotic in L3 Polish at T4, three had target-like pronunciations from T1 onwards (DIMO03, LYBO29, MESC03). SYLÜ08 produced both [r] and [ɾ] at T1, varied between [r], [ɾ] and [ʁ] at T2 and returned to producing [r] and [ɾ] at T4. DOSC23 shows substantial variability in realising the Polish rhotic at T1, including [ɾ], the voiceless velar fricative [x] and a combined [ʁ/x] sound, but then consistently realised it as [ʁ] at both T2 and T4. For both SYLÜ08 and DOSC23 thus there is cross-linguistic influence from the L1 at one point in time reflecting the competition of the different realisation of the rhotic in their languages, which formed the basis for dynamic developments at later stages. All of the other multilinguals' pronunciation of the Polish rhotic is still variable and includes non-target forms at T4, hence reflecting a dynamic, non-stable state in their development.

Zooming into the variability at the micro-level and mid-term development, Figure 6 displays min-max graphs for the production of /w/ in L2 English and L3 Polish by SYLÜ08 across the eighteen weeks of dense data collection. It shows that, overall, variability in the accuracy of producing /w/ at each weekly data collection point is higher in L2 English than in L3 Polish. Only at around week 15 of the observation period does the production of English /w/ stabilise.

For ROGI18, by contrast, more variability in the production of /w/ occurs in L3 Polish than in L2 English (see Figure 7). She produces English /w/ most accurately at the start of the observation period, which is then followed by some weeks of increased variability that diminishes again at week 14 but ultimately returns. No clear picture arises as to how this variability at the micro level may affect the speakers' mid/long-term development.

H3. Extreme variability at one point in time signals (upcoming) major developmental changes.

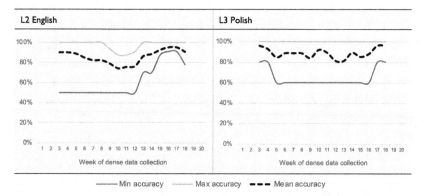

Figure 6 Accuracy of production of /w/ in L2 English and L3 Polish by SYLÜ08 across the eighteen weeks of dense data collection.

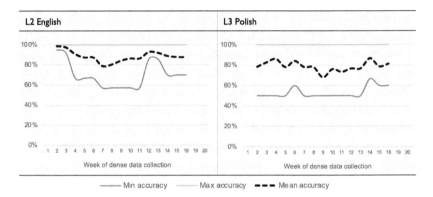

Figure 7 Accuracy of production of /w/ in L2 English and L3 Polish by ROGI18 across the eighteen weeks of dense data collection.

As can be seen in Figure 5, two multilinguals show extreme variability (80 per cent) in their rhotic productions at some point in time: COSC26 in L3 Polish at T2 and CHSC09 in L3 Polish at T1. CHSC09 realises the five Polish words containing a rhotic with the L1 sounds uvular fricative [ʁ] (twice) and uvular trill [ʀ] as well as the combined sounds [k/ʀ] and [x/ʀ] at T1. At T2, she produces three realisations: [ʀ] (three times), [x] (once) and [ʁ] (four times). At T4, however, her Polish rhotics show only two different realisations, [ʁ] six times and [ʀ] three times. While for CHSC09 the extreme variability of rhotic productions at T1 might be interpreted as heralding an upcoming stabilisation of the system, this hypothesis does not hold for COSC26's development. She produces three different realisations ([ʁ] four times as well as [v] and [k/x] once each) in the six Polish words containing a rhotic at T1 and then shows extreme variability at T2, when she realises the five Polish words containing rhotics with the English approximant [ɹ] twice as well as [w], [ʀ] and [ʁ] once each. At T2, thus, her realisations of the Polish rhotic consist of both L2 and L1 sounds but no target-like sounds. At T4, however, she produces the seven Polish words containing rhotics with a target-like trill [r] four times, as well as [ʁ], [ɹ] and [l] once each. Her subsystem thus has not stabilised after ten months of learning Polish but now contains L1, L2 and L3 realisations of the rhotic. The high variability in her productions observed at T2 can still be interpreted as signalling a major developmental step insofar as her productions of the Polish rhotic at T4 for the first time include some target-like realisations.

To identify possible major developmental changes in the production of the other features also tested in the study, we performed change point analyses of

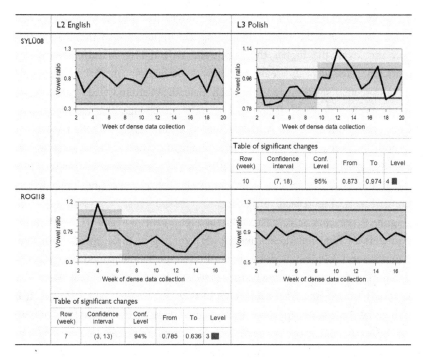

Figure 8 Change point analyses of vowel reduction ratio in L2 English and L3 Polish by SYLÜ08 (eighteen weeks of dense data collection) and ROGI18 (sixteen weeks of dense data collection).

the weekly collected L2 and L3 vowel reduction and final obstruent (de)voicing by SYLÜ08, ROGI18 and REBA03. Figure 8 displays the identified phase shifts or lack thereof for the ratio of vowel duration in stressed/ unstressed vowel pairs (values of around 1 indicate the same length) in two speakers. The two lines in the graph are control limits which represent the maximum range over which the values are expected to vary assuming no change has occurred. Points outside the control limits indicate that a change has occurred, visually represented by the dark grey shifts in the background, in which case the accompanying table provides further information describing the change(s).

SYLÜ08 demonstrated no developmental shift in realising vowel reduction in his L2 English in the observation period, as evidenced by the absence of any dark grey shifts in the background; the L2 vowel ratio values still fluctuate on a weekly basis. He did, however, change his realisation of unstressed vowels in relation to the stressed vowels in his L3 Polish at around week 10: prior to the change, the average vowel reduction ratio yielded a value of 0.87, while after the change it was 0.97. This change occurred with a 95 per cent confidence and level 4 was associated with it, indicating the importance of the change (the lower the level, the higher the importance). ROGI18, in turn, showed no significant changes in realising vowel reduction in L3 Polish but a developmental shift in her L2 English instead. At around week 7, her vowel reduction ratio dropped from 0.78 to 0.64, a change that occurred with 94 per cent confidence and was detected on a third pass of the data (level 3). For both speakers, the identified developmental shifts exhibited a target-like direction. Analyses of respective shifts as per standard deviation changes yielded no significant results, which suggests that they were not preceded by extreme levels of increased variability.

Figure 9 presents selected results for significant changes in the duration parameters of final obstruent (underlying) voicing in three speakers in their L2 English or L3 Polish. It shows that all three speakers changed their consonant duration (rather than vowel or consonant burst duration that were also measured) in realising final obstruents in their L2 English or L3 Polish. It is notable that these shifts approach the expected target in that voiced realisations are to be expected to show shorter consonant duration than devoiced realisations (as manifested in REBA03's production of shorter voiced final obstruents in English, and SYLÜ08's and ROGI18's production of prolonged devoiced final obstruents in Polish).

SYLÜ08 evidenced one significant shift in his realisation of L3 consonant duration (with 99 per cent confidence, level 1 change) at around the same time as his realisation of vowel reduction changed (see Figure 8), which coincides with his move to Poland for a stay abroad. Interestingly, REBA03 evidenced two significant shifts in her production of L2 English consonants in that she lengthened her word-final obstruents from around week 10 of the data collection (97 per cent confidence, level 1 change) but five weeks later returned to her original manner of realising the sounds (the average length stabilising at 0.14 ms; 94 per cent confidence, level 2 change), which is suggestive of the speaker's preferred, 'attractor' length. The third speaker, ROGI18, significantly changed her production of L3 Polish word-final obstruents in terms of both consonant duration and burst duration at around week 10 of the data collection (with 95 per cent and 97 per cent confidence, respectively, both changes identified at level 1). An inspection of change point analyses for standard deviation and the identified developmental shifts indicated no significant results. There is thus little evidence in the present dense data on vowel reduction and final obstruent (de)voicing for extreme variability as an index of upcoming major developmental changes for the three speakers.

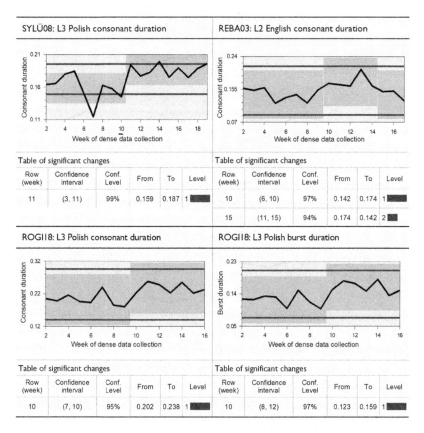

Figure 9 Selected change point analyses for final obstruent (de)voicing in L2 English or L3 Polish by SYLÜ08 (eighteen weeks of data collection), REBA03 and ROGI18 (sixteen weeks of data collection).

H4. Different phonetic and phonological features develop in interaction with each other.

Figures 10 and 11 display the accuracy of producing both /w/ and the rhotics across the four data points for each speaker. A clear interaction can be seen between the development of the two sounds in their L2 English for the four speakers shown on the top row, DIMO03, REBA03, JUEB20 and SMSC15. Although on different levels of accuracy (e.g., ceiling performance for DIMO03 for both sounds but relatively low accuracy for /ɹ/ produced by JUEB20), the production of those two sounds for these four speakers show parallel increases and decreases of accuracy from T1 to T4. No such relationship could be found for the remaining twelve speakers, where the accuracy of their L2 English /w/ and /ɹ/ production seems to develop independently,

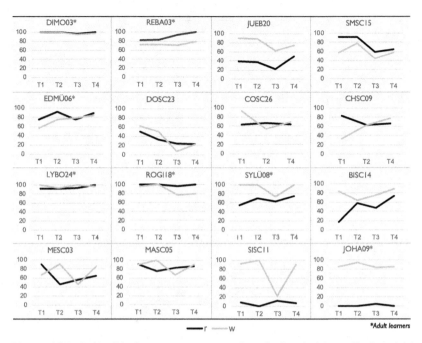

Figure 10 Relationship between accuracy of producing /w/ (grey line) and /ɹ/
(black line) in L2 English for the sixteen speakers.

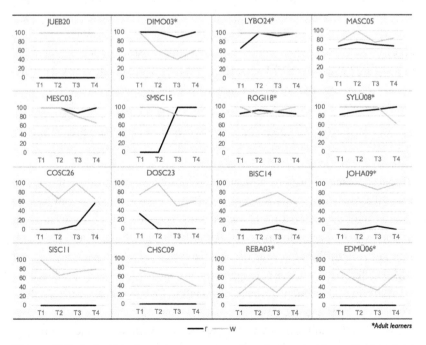

Figure 11 Relationship between accuracy of producing /w/ (grey line) and /r/
(black line) in L3 Polish for the sixteen speakers.

though perhaps one might suggest some linkage between the two sounds for SYLÜ08.

There is little evidence for these sixteen speakers exhibiting parallel development in producing /w/ and /r/ in their L3 Polish (see Figure 11). Many speakers never pronounce Polish /r/ correctly during the first ten months of learning this language, especially those shown on the last row, SISC11, CHSC09, REBA03 and EDMÜ06, and also JUEB20 on the top row, while BISC14 and JOHA09 only produce one token correctly at T3. Some tendencies for parallel developments of the production of the two sounds are evident for DIMO03 from T3 and LYBO24 at T4, but in general the two sounds do not develop together in the L3 Polish.

H5. The perception and production of speech sounds co-evolve.

Tables 2–5 show how many individual learners evidenced different patterns of a perception-production relationship for L2 and L3 rhotics and /w/ at each of the main testing times, as well as across the testing times (the last column in the tables). The categorisation of these patterns is based on the calculation of within-subject effect size (Cohen's d) for perception and production differences in mean scores ($d \leq 0.7$ = small to no effects, $d \geq 0.7$ = medium effects and $d \geq 1.0$ = large effects; cf. Plonsky & Oswald, 2014). That is, a small within-subject effect size was interpreted as suggesting no meaningful difference between the production and perception scores and thus some evidence for a co-evolution of the skills for a learner ('perception = production'). Medium and large within-subject effect sizes suggested a precedence of one skill over another for a learner (either 'perception > production' or 'production > perception'). If one or both of the skills equalled or fell below a 50 per cent accuracy threshold, this was interpreted as pointing at a 'dissociation' between a learner's perception

Table 2 Total number of learners showing a particular type of relationship between perception and production of L2 rhotic sounds at each testing time.

	L2 rhotic sounds				
	T1 (n=16)	T2 (n=16)	T3 (n=13)	T4 (n=16)	T1–T4
perception = production	11	8	5	10	6
perception > production	4	3	2	2	0
dissociation	1	5	6	4	3

The last column excludes those participants who showed an inconsistent pattern of perception-production development across the testing times.

Table 3 Total number of learners showing a particular type of relationship between perception and production of L3 rhotic sounds at each testing time.

	L3 rhotic sounds				
	T1 (no data)	T2 (n=16)	T3 (n=15)	T4 (n=16)	T2–T4
perception = production		6	6	6	6
perception > production		0	0	1	0
dissociation		10	9	9	9

The last column excludes those participants who showed an inconsistent pattern of perception-production development across the testing times.

Table 4 Total number of learners showing a particular type of relationship between perception and production of L2 /w/ at each testing time.

	L2 /w/				
	T1 (n=16)	T2 (n=16)	T3 (n=14)	T4 (n=16)	T1–T4
perception = production	13	12	11	13	10
dissociation	3	4	3	3	0

The last column excludes those participants who showed an inconsistent pattern of perception-production development across the testing times.

Table 5 Total number of learners showing a particular type of relationship between perception and production of L3 /w/ at each testing time.

	L3 /w/				
	T1 (n=16)	T2 (n=16)	T3 (n=15)	T4 (n=16)	T1–T4
perception = production	13	14	11	14	10
dissociation	3	2	4	2	1

The last column excludes those participants who showed an inconsistent pattern of perception-production development across the testing times.

and production, suggesting lack of ability and hence little direct relationship. For an overview of individual learner trajectories and perception-production relationships, see the Appendix.

As shown in Table 2, overall, the learners in this study perceived L2 English rhotics equally accurately as they produced the sounds (eleven learners at T1, eight learners at T2, five learners at T3 and ten learners at T4). Six learners (five adults and one adolescent) showed a consistent alignment in perceiving and producing L2 English rhotics across the four testing times (note that the total count across the four testing times, provided in the last column in Tables 2–5, may differ from the number of participants as not all of the learners evidenced a consistent pattern of a perception-production relationship across the main testing times). The young learners tended to manifest more varied patterns at each testing point, with two of them evidencing a consistent dissociation of their perception and production of L2 rhotics, i.e., one or both of their skills in the L2 showed an accuracy level equal or below the 50 per cent threshold. As shown in Table 3, this latter pattern was predominantly found for both learner groups in their L3 Polish: nine out of the sixteen learners consistently perceived alveolar trills fairly accurately (as tested in the FC task) but were not able to produce them accurately. Yet six learners performed equally well in both modalities in their L3 across the testing times, suggesting a co-evolution of their L3 perception and production skills.

The same analyses concerning the perception-production link for rhotic sounds were also carried out for the labiovelar approximant /w/. Tables 4 and 5 show that the two modalities developed in alignment for the majority of the adolescent and adult learners for this phonological feature, in both their L2 English and L3 Polish. For example, ten learners perceived L2/L3 /w/ as accurately as they produced the sound across the four testing times. If a dissociation relationship was identified, this was usually a scenario of a learner producing /w/ in their L2/L3 more accurately than perceiving it (as tested in the ABX task), with one or both of the skills equalling or falling below the 50 per cent threshold though.

Overall, our data suggests that perception and production of speech sounds tend to co-evolve, although the strength of the link can be moderated by the phonetic characteristics of the sound concerned and the stage of language learning.

H6. The developmental relationship between a learner's foreign languages is initially competitive and subsequently supportive, which changes with proficiency.

Figure 12 shows the relationship between the production of /w/ by SYLÜ08 in L2 English and L3 Polish as a moving correlation. It shows that in the first ten weeks the relationship is a competitive one, in that his production of the sound is negatively related in his two foreign languages (r = between −0.20 and −0.80), but the relationship turns into a supportive one from week 13 to 15 (r = between 0.60 and 0.80).

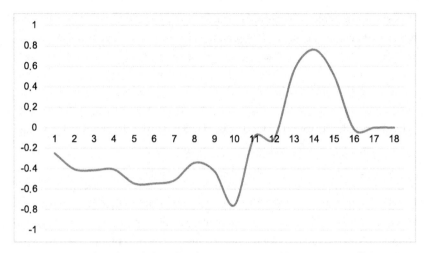

Figure 12 Moving correlation for the production of /w/ in L2 English and L3 Polish by speaker SYLÜ08.

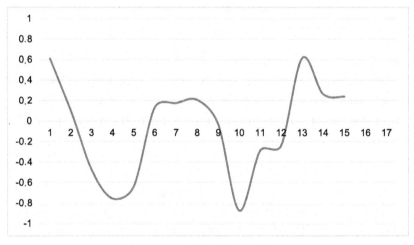

Figure 13 Moving correlation for the production of vowel reduction in L2 English and L3 Polish by speaker SYLÜ08.

This is in contrast to the relationship found for the production of vowel reduction in L2 English and L3 Polish by the same speaker, which is far more fluctuating (see Figure 13). In the first two weeks as well as weeks 6 to 8 of the observation period, vowel reduction in both of his languages develops in alignment, i.e., the vowel reduction ratio is positively related in his two foreign languages (r = between 0.20 and 0.60), while for weeks 3 to 5 it is negatively related (r = between −0.20 and −0.80). An increased distinction between vowel

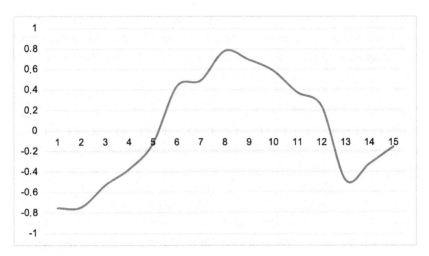

Figure 14 Moving correlation for the production of /w/ in L2 English and L3 Polish by ROGI18.

reduction in L2 and L3 can again be seen for weeks 9 to 12 (r = between −0.20 and −0.80) before it diminishes again towards the end of the observation period.

Figure 14 displays the moving correlation for the production of /w/ in L2 English and L3 Polish for ROGI18. Like for SYLÜ08 for this phonological feature, an initially competitive relationship between the two languages turns into a primarily supportive one (weeks 6 to 12). However, it returns to being competitive again towards the end of the observation period. Thus, for both speakers and for the production of /w/, the increase of proficiency in L3 Polish does seem to go hand in hand with a more supportive relationship between the learners' two foreign languages, which tends to be more competitive at earlier stages. However, the production of vowel reduction in the two languages appears to have a rather more complex relationship, vacillating several times between competitive and supportive.

6 Discussion

It was one aim of this study to describe the phonetic and phonological development of multilingual speakers within the framework of CDST and to thereby both test some of the main tenets of this theory and contribute to it. Our results showed that, as hypothesised in H1, learning trends in phonetic and phonological development based on group scores do not model well the learning processes of individual learners. Confirming findings by van Dijk et al. (2011) for the development of grammar, our data also showed, for each of the four analysed phonetic and phonological features and for both modalities, production and perception, that the learning trajectories of individual learners vary substantially and cannot be represented by the trend that results from calculating group mean values. As proposed within the framework of CDST, speaker variation should thus be treated as a meaningful aspect of language development in L2/L3 research and group means need to be interpreted with care. Moreover, the individual learning trajectories in our data show that development in most cases is non-linear: the accuracy in perception and production of all analysed phonetic and phonological features shows drops across the ten months of the observation period for many of the sixteen learners. The results thus complement the PAM-L2 and the SLM/SLM-r, which propose a continuous, slow refinement of L2 learners' perception of phonetic differences between their L1 and L2, with a more refined insight into the developmental dynamics of the process. While the upward trend might apply on a very general level of language development (i.e., the macro level; see Hammarberg, 2017), it does not hold entirely true for the actual developmental process at close inspection, which instead involves a back-and-forth progress. The results of the present study thus support the CDST conceptualisation of the language learning process as dynamic, non-linear, variable and highly individual.

The results further show that variability exists not only across different learners and their processes of multilingual language development but also within learners at different phases of their phonetic and phonological development. With the second hypothesis, we wanted to explore a possible relationship between learners' variability at the micro level and their long-term developments by comparing the variability of production at one point in time (the micro perspective reflecting single events of language use; see Hammarberg, 2017) with mid-term and long-term development. For both the production of the rhotics and the production of /w/, individual learners showed dynamic phases with increased variability and cross-linguistic influence from their other languages as well as phases of relative stability with less variability. As in Hammarberg's (2017) study, there was substantial variation across the sixteen learners in terms of both whether and when variability at the individual data collection points occurred and whether a period of stabilisation could be observed. Yet, no conclusive patterns were found that point towards the role variation at the micro level plays for long-term developmental trends: alternating phases of variability and relative stability in the pronunciation of individual speech sounds were observed for the learners' L1 German, L2 English and L3 Polish, irrespective of the fact that they were beginners in Polish and much more advanced learners of English. Furthermore, some learners never showed any variability at any of the data collection points and produced the speech sounds in the same (target or non-target) way. Given an observation period of only ten months and a period of dense data collection covering only eighteen weeks, our data might not have been optimally suited for capturing long-term trends. Thus, more research is needed to explore the relationship between variability at the micro level and long-term developments.

Another aspect of variability and its relationship with the dynamicity of the phonetic and phonological learning process that was explored in this study concerns the hypothesis that extreme variability at one point in time signals (upcoming) major developmental changes, as suggested by van Dijk and van Geert (2007) and Evans and Larsen-Freeman (2020). No clear evidence for this hypothesis could be found: while the analysis of the four observation times spread across the first ten months of learning the L3 Polish showed that extreme variability does occur, such as five different realisations of one speech sound at one point in time, it is difficult to link them to major developmental changes. For one learner, extreme variability preceded a restructuring of the L3 Polish subsystem that then included realisations from the L1, L2 and L3; for another learner, extreme variability was followed by a phase of reduced variability. However, due to the fact that the data collection points were spread out over several weeks or even months, which was especially true for the L1 data collection, it is not possible to say what developments occurred between them and what effect the extreme variability may have had. Yet, even in the dense data that included data collected at weekly intervals, no clear evidence was found for increased variability before developmental changes. Future research will have to investigate whether this applies only to phonetic and phonological development or whether this seriously questions the suggestion by van Dijk and van Geert (2007) and Evans and Larsen-Freeman (2020) that high variability indicates developmental changes. In this connection, it will be important in future research to carefully consider the criteria that characterise patterns of discontinuity in the development of a particular feature under scrutiny (cf. van Dijk & van Geert, 2007). The present results suggest that extreme variability, understood as an unexpectedly large, local peak in the data, is not a prerequisite for major developmental changes.

This study traced the development of various phonetic and phonological features and, with the fourth hypothesis, aimed at exploring whether these develop in interaction with each other or rather independently. To this end, the development of the pronunciation of /w/ and the rhotics was compared in the learners' L2 English and also their L3 Polish. The results suggest that the learning of the pronunciation of these two speech sounds proceeds largely independently and thus stands in contrast to findings by Yu and Lowie (2019), who found an interaction between the development of oral complexity and accuracy in their L1 Chinese learners' L2 English that developed from an initially competitive relationship to a supportive one. The discrepancy between our findings and theirs might be explained by the fact that individual speech sounds form independent subsystems within a learner's phonology, while grammatical complexity and accuracy in oral language production depend more on each other. Yet the results once more underline the substantial inter-variability across the multilingual learners and suggest a possible role for language proficiency. For four of the learners, parallel developments between the production of /w/ and /ɹ/ were found in their L2 English only, pointing at closer interconnections in a relatively well-established subsystem for these learners and for speech sounds that are phonetically related.

The fifth hypothesis aimed to explore the relationship between the perception and production of individual speech sounds. According to the SLM-r (Flege & Bohn, 2021), the two modalities co-evolve, implying that there is a close relationship between perception and production development, while the PAM-L2 postulates no direct link between them. Our results show that the two skills do tend to develop in alignment, although the strength of the relationship is moderated by the speech sound as well as the stage of language learning. The different L2 and L3 rhotic sounds investigated in this study arguably present different degrees of perceptual saliency and articulatory challenge than /w/ does (Archibald, 2009; Catford, 2001; Colantoni & Steele, 2008), which may explain the more varied patterns of a perception-production relationship for the rhotics than for the labiovelar approximant. It is also to be recalled that /w/ is a sound shared in both the L2 and the L3 of the learners in this study, which may have facilitated the multilinguals' ability to perceive and to produce the familiar phoneme in their newly learnt L3. Our results further suggest that the more established the phonological subsystem of a learner, in this study the L2 in relation to the L3, the greater the likelihood of a close relationship between the development of the two skills, which is in line with studies that have reported a stronger positive correlation between perception and production with increases in L2 proficiency (Cardoso, 2011; Hanulíková et al., 2012). In a broader sense, our findings are thus in agreement with the CDST's theorising on the interconnected nature of learner subsystems (perception and production of speech sounds in this case) and on the potentially competing demands from the different parts of the language subsystems (de Bot et al., 2007) such as the regulation of sensory and motor processes, activation of the lexicon and syntax, which will be especially operative in the beginning stages of learning a foreign language. Our analyses of individual learner performance show yet again that the degree of correspondence between perception and production as well as any changes in that correspondence over time differ for individual multilinguals.

The present results clearly confirm that the languages of multilingual speakers interact as already documented in numerous previous studies (see Section 1). This interaction is reflected in the intra-speaker variability that was observed for many learners in all of their languages when they realise, for example, the rhotics in their L3 Polish variably with the L1 German rhotics [ʀ] and [ʁ] and/or the L2 English rhotic [ɹ] or even combinations and newly created mixed sounds such as [x/ʀ]. The last hypotheses aimed to explore the relationship between the multilingual speakers' languages with a longitudinal perspective and tested whether the developmental relationship between a learner's foreign languages is initially competitive and subsequently support-ive. This type of interaction had rarely been tested across a multilingual speaker's different languages (cf. Huang et al., 2020) but was found for different features of oral language development by Yu and Lowie (2019) within the learners' target language. In our densely collected data, we compared the accuracy of the production of various speech sounds in the learners' L2 English and L3 Polish and found different patterns for different speech sounds. There is some suggestion that, for the production of /w/, which represents a shared novel feature in the learners' L2 and L3, with increasing proficiency in the L3 Polish a more supportive relationship between the L2 and L3 sets in, though it tended to be more competitive at earlier stages. However, again the time window captured by our analysis might have been too small for stable conclusions as shown in the data on vowel reduction: for this phonological process, whose realisation is dissimilar in the learners' two foreign languages, the L2 English and the L3 Polish have a rather more complex relationship that changes several times between being competitive and supportive over the course of the eighteen weeks of dense data collection. It will be important in future research to expand on the range of investigated features across a multilingual speaker's languages to capture (and measure) the range of cross-linguistic similarity types possibly mediating the type of a developmental relationship between the learners' languages.

7 Conclusion

We have shown that employing longitudinal and dense data with a focus on individual learners contributes important insights for describing and under-standing multilingual phonetic and phonological development and that this approach can complement traditional, more product-oriented research designs. The new methods presented in Section 3 and applied in our own study are more suited to showing dynamic development of phonology and phonetics in terms of the interaction between different features as well as the interplay of the different languages than traditional average scores and group comparisons. Moreover, a focus on individual learners as well as on developments in small time windows brings to light both the variability across learners and the individual and dynamic process of their pronunciation learning.

The revised SLM-r (Flege & Bohn, 2021), with its new orientation towards investigating how the phonetic systems of individuals reorganise over time, would seem to be in line with our proposed avenue of research into multilingual phonetic and phonological learning. Also, the model's assumption of L1 and L2 sharing the same phonetic space may well be extendable to L3 speech learning contexts: all of the multilingual's languages share a common phonetic space and are thus subject to (dynamic) interactions in the course of the learner's development of speech perception and production. In a similar vein, it is to be expected that perceptual assimilation of native and non-native sounds and sound contrasts as theorised in both the SLM/SLM-r (Flege, 1995; Flege & Bohn, 2021) and the PAM/PAM-L2 (Best, 1995; Best & Tyler, 2007) works in like manner, the difference being that L3 sounds and sound contrasts can be perceptually associated with either L1, L2 or both languages by L3 learners. The micro-level scrutiny of such a multilingual phonetic and phonological development in individual learners will nevertheless deserve yet greater scholarly attention and focus.

Our study also showed the limitations of a comprehensive, process-oriented approach to studying pronunciation learning by multilinguals. The inclusion of both production and perception data from three languages for each learner in a longitudinal research design naturally limited the number of phonetic and phonological features that could be investigated. Especially with younger learners, the number of tasks they are required to perform at each data collection point needs to be limited to avoid fatigue and a subsequent withdrawal from the study.

Our study constitutes only a first step in the investigation of pronunciation development of multilingual learners. We hope that many further studies using dense data and a CDST framework will follow to shed more light on this complex issue. Our study showed that an even larger time window for the dense data collection as well as its commencement earlier in the L3 learning process might have provided richer data and greater insight into the complex and dynamic process of pronunciation learning. In particular, in this way it might be better understood how individual learner productions and perception at the micro level contribute to long-term learning at the macro level. Finally, an important direction of future research will be to integrate quantitative data with qualitative (biographical) data in order to not only characterise the process of an individual multilingual's phonetic and phonological development and changes thereof but also to better understand the underlying environmental and affective reasons for such developmental changes.

Appendix

Within-subject effect size (Cohen's *d*) for perception-production differences as per individual learners, languages and testing times ($d \leq 0.7$ = little to no effects, $d \geq 0.7$ = medium effects and $d \geq 1.0$ = large effects). The effect size value of infinity was yielded for cases of 100 per cent accuracy in perception and 0 per cent accuracy in production.

Table A1 Individual learner trajectories concerning the relationship between perception and production of L2 English rhotics.

	L2 English rhotics			
	T1	**T2**	**T3**	**T4**
BISC14	dissociation (2.07)	percept = product (1.17)	dissociation (1.02)	percept > product (0.85)
CHSC09	percept = product (0.62)	percept > product (1.05)	–	percept > product (0.98)
COSC26	percept = product (0.63)	percept = product (0.59)	–	percept = product (0.12)
DIMO03*	percept = product (0)	percept = product (0)	percept = product (0.30)	percept = product (0)
DOSC23	percept = product (0.40)	dissociation (0.59)	dissociation (2.41)	dissociation (2.53)
EDMÜ06*	percept = product (0.38)	percept = product (0.30)	percept = product (0.17)	percept = product (0.06)
JOHA09*	dissociation (infinity)	dissociation (infinity)	dissociation (6.31)	dissociation (infinity)
JUEB20	dissociation (0.90)	dissociation (0.95)	dissociation (1.39)	dissociation (1.39)
LYBO24*	percept = product (0)	percept = product (0.24)	percept = product (0.07)	percept = product (0)
MASC05	percept = product (0)	percept > product (0.79)	percept = product (0.65)	percept = product (0.59)
MESC03	percept = product (0)	dissociation (1.05)	percept > product (1.25)	percept = product (0.63)
REBA03*	percept = product (0.26)	percept = product (0.63)	–	percept = product (0)
ROGI18*	percept = product (0.47)	percept = product (0.46)	percept = product (0.30)	percept = product (0)
SISC11	dissociation (0.28)	dissociation (infinity)	dissociation (3.81)	dissociation (2.85)
SMSC15	percept = product (0.30)	percept = product (0.31)	dissociation (0.82)	percept = product (0.12)
SYLÜ08*	percept > product (1.22)	percept > product (0.91)	percept > product (1.10)	percept = product (0.12)

*Adult learners

Appendix

Table A2 Individual learner trajectories concerning the relationship between perception and production of L3 Polish rhotics.

	L3 Polish rhotics		
	T2	**T3**	**T4**
BISC14	dissociation (1.70)	dissociation (1.95)	dissociation (1.66)
CHSC09	dissociation (2.06)	dissociation 1.66)	dissociation (1.64)
COSC26	dissociation (2.06)	–	percept > product (0.76)
DIMO03*	percept = product (0)	percept = product (0.51)	percept = product (0)
DOSC23	dissociation (2.06)	dissociation (2.69)	dissociation (2.69)
EDMÜ06*	dissociation (2.69)	dissociation (infinity)	dissociation (infinity)
JOHA09*	dissociation (infinity)	dissociation (5.06)	dissociation (infinity)
JUEB20	dissociation (2.69)	dissociation (2.06)	dissociation (2.06)
LYBO24*	percept = product (0)	percept = product (0.35)	percept = product (0)
MASC05	percept = product (0.11)	percept = product (0)	percept = product (0.30)
MESC03	percept = product (0)	percept = product (0.51)	percept = product (0)
REBA03*	dissociation (infinity)	dissociation (infinity)	dissociation (infinity)
ROGI18*	percept = product (0.07)	percept = product (0.51)	percept = product (0.61)
SISC11	dissociation (1.36)	dissociation (2.06)	dissociation (1.11)
SMSC15	dissociation (0.96)	dissociation (2.06)	dissociation (2.69)
SYLÜ08*	percept = product (0.63)	percept = product (0.60)	percept = product (0)

*Adult learners

Table A3 Individual learner trajectories concerning the relationship between perception and production of L2 English /w/.

	T1	T2	T3	T4
		L2 English /w/		
BISC14	percept = product (0.45)	percept = product (0.11)	percept = product (0.06)	percept = product (0.67)
CHSC09	percept = product (0.44)	percept = product (0.01)	–	percept = product (0.37)
COSC26	percept = product (0.54)	percept = product (0.02)	–	percept = product (0.26)
DIMO03*	percept = product (0.05)	percept = product (0.67)	percept = product (0.63)	percept = product (0.27)
DOSC23	percept = product (0)	percept = product (0.15)	dissociation (1.48)	dissociation (0.59)
EDMÜ06*	percept = product (0.03)	percept = product (0.10)	percept = product (0.13)	percept = product (0.23)
JOHA09*	percept = product (0.38)	percept = product (0.39)	percept = product (0.10)	percept = product (0.12)
JUEB20	dissociation (1.43)	dissociation (1.07)	percept = product (0.10)	dissociation (0.51)
LYBO24*	percept = product (0.40)	percept = product (0.38)	percept = product (0.23)	percept = product (0.17)
MASC05	dissociation (1.11)	dissociation (1.92)	percept = product (0.43)	dissociation (1.0)
MESC03	percept = product (0.08)	percept = product (0.68)	dissociation (0.82)	percept = product (0.50)
REBA03*	percept = product (0.25)	percept = product (0.37)	percept = product (0.23)	percept = product (0.18)
ROGI18*	percept = product (0.18)	percept = product (0.20)	percept = product (0.26)	percept = product (0.20)
SISC11	dissociation (1.14)	dissociation (1.03)	dissociation (0.51)	percept = product (0.59)
SMSC15	percept = product (0.16)	dissociation (0.80)	percept = product (0.47)	percept = product (0.37)
SYLÜ08*	percept = product (0.44)	percept = product (0.31)	percept = product (0.68)	percept = product (0.41)

*Adult learners

Table A4 Individual learner trajectories concerning the relationship between perception and production of L3 Polish /w/.

	T1	T2	T3	T4
		L3 Polish /w/		
BISC14	dissociation (0.76)	percept = product (0.32)	percept = product (0.10)	percept = product (0.52)
CHSC09	percept = product (0.38)	dissociation (1.00)	percept = product (0.51)	dissociation (0.94)
COSC26	percept = product (0.22)	percept = product (0.07)	–	percept = product (0.23)
DIMO03*	percept = product (0.11)	percept = product (0.46)	percept = product (0.65)	percept = product (0.24)
DOSC23	dissociation (0.76)	percept = product (0.61)	dissociation (0.56)	percept = product (0.64)
EDMÜ06*	percept = product (0.04)	percept = product (0.12)	percept = product (0.43)	percept = product (0.13)
JOHA09*	percept = product (0.50)	percept = product (0.19)	percept = product (0.61)	percept = product (0.06)
JUEB20	dissociation (0.04)	dissociation (1.17)	dissociation (1.00)	dissociation (0.81)
LYBO24*	percept = product (0.05)	percept = product (0.13)	percept = product (0.01)	percept = product (0.31)
MASC05	percept = product (0.19)	percept = product (0.07)	dissociation (0.99)	percept = product (0.68)
MESC03	percept = product (0.32)	percept = product (0.31)	percept = product (0.22)	percept = product (0.18)
REBA03*	percept = product (0.04)	percept = product (0.11)	percept = product (0.61)	percept = product (0.13)
ROGI18*	percept = product (0.16)	percept = product (0.12)	percept = product (0.22)	percept = product (0.03)
SISC11	percept = product (0.61)	percept = product (0.26)	percept = product (0.14)	percept = product (0.04)
SMSC15	percept = product (0.43)	percept = product (0.39)	percept = product (0.15)	percept = product (0.15)
SYLÜ08*	percept = product (0.42)	percept = product (0.39)	percept = product (0.81)	percept = product (0.46)

*Adult learners

References

Amengual, M., Meredith, L., & Panelli, T. (2019). Static and dynamic phonetic interactions in the L2 and L3 acquisition of Japanese velar voiceless stops. In S. Calhoun, P. Escudero, M. Tabain, & P. Warren (Eds.), *Proceedings of the 19th International Congress of Phonetic Sciences* (pp. 964–8). Australasian Speech Science and Technology Association Inc.

Ankerstein, C. A., & Morschett, R. (2013). Do you hear what I hear? A comparison of phoneme perception in native and Saarlandian German nonnative speakers of English. *Saarland Working Papers in Linguistics, 4*, 1–8.

Antoniou, M., Liang, E., Ettlinger, M., & Wong, P. (2015). The bilingual advantage in phonetic learning. *Bilingualism: Language and Cognition, 18* (4), 683–95.

Aoki, R., & Nishihara, F. (2013). Sound feature interference between two second languages: An expansion of the feature hypothesis to the multilingual situation in SLA. In C. Cathcart, I.-H. Chen, G. Finley et al. (Eds.), *Proceedings of the 37th Annual Meeting of the Berkeley Linguistics Society* (pp. 18–32). Berkeley Linguistics Society.

Aoyama, K., Guion, S. G., Flege, J. E., Yamada, T., & Akahane-Yamada, R. (2008). The first years in an L2-speaking environment: A comparison of Japanese children and adults learning American English. *IRAL: International Review of Applied Linguistics in Language Teaching, 46*(1), 61–90. https://doi.org/10.1515/IRAL.2008.003.

Archibald, J. (2009). Phonological feature re-assembly and the importance of phonetic cues. *Second Language Research, 25*(2), 231–3. https://doi.org/10.1177/0267658308100284.

Beckmann, E. (2012). 'A gup of dea, please': Crosslinguistic influence in English and German word-initial stops produced by German L3 learners of Dutch. *Dutch Journal of Applied Linguistics, 1*(2), 252–62. https://doi.org/10.1075/dujal.1.2.06bec.

Best, C. T. (1995). A direct realist view of cross-language speech perception. In W. Strange (Ed.), *Speech perception and linguistic experience: Issues in cross-language research* (pp. 171–204). York Press.

Best, C. T., & Tyler, M. D. (2007). Nonnative and second-language speech perception: Commonalities and complementarities. In O.-S. Bohn & M. J. Munro (Eds.), *Language experience in second language speech learning: In honor of James Emil Flege* (pp. 13–34). John Benjamins Publishing.

Boersma, P., & Weenink, D. (2021). *Praat: Doing phonetics by computer* (6.2.03) [Computer software].

Cabrelli, J. (2016). Testing the phonological permeability hypothesis: L3 phonological effects on L1 versus L2 systems. *International Journal of Bilingualism, 21*(6), 698–717. https://doi.org/10.1177/1367006916637287.

Cabrelli, J., & Pichan, C. (2019). Initial phonological transfer in L3 Brazilian Portuguese and Italian. *Linguistic Approaches to Bilingualism, 11*(2), 131–67. https://doi.org/10.1075/lab.18048.cab.

Cabrelli, J., & Rothman, J. (2010). On L3 acquisition and phonological permeability: A new test case for debates on the mental representation of non-native phonological systems. *IRAL: International Review of Applied Linguistics in Language Teaching, 48*(2–3), 275–96. https://doi.org/10.1515/iral.2010.012.

Cardoso, W. (2011). The development of coda perception in second language phonology: A variationist perspective. *Second Language Research, 27*(4), 433–65. https://doi.org/10.1177/0267658311413540.

Catford, J. C. (2001). *A practical introduction to phonetics* (2nd ed). Oxford University Press.

Cebrian, J. (2000). Transferability and productivity of L1 rules in Catalan–English interlanguage. *Studies in Second Language Acquisition, 22*(1), 1–26. https://doi.org/10.1017/S0272263100001017.

Chan, H., Verspoor, M., & Vahtrick, L. (2015). Dynamic development in speaking versus writing in identical twins. *Language Learning, 65*(2), 298–325. https://doi.org/10.1111/lang.12107.

Colantoni, L., & Steele, J. (2008). Integrating articulatory constraints into models of second language phonological acquisition. *Applied Psycholinguistics, 29*(3), 489–534. https://doi.org/10.1017/S014271640 8080223.

Colantoni, L., Steele, J., & Escudero, P. (2015). *Second language speech: Theory and practice*. Cambridge University Press.

De Angelis, G. (2007). *Third or additional language acquisition*. Multilingual Matters. https://doi.org/10.21832/9781847690050.

de Bot, K. (2012). Rethinking multilingual processing: From a static to a dynamic approach. In J. Cabrelli, S. Flynn, & J. Rothman (Eds.), *Third language acquisition in adulthood* (Vol. 46, pp. 79–94). John Benjamins Publishing. https://doi.org/10.1075/sibil.46.07bot.

de Bot, K., & Larsen-Freeman, D. (2011). Researching second language development from a dynamic systems theory perspective. In M. Verspoor, K. de Bot & W. Lowie (Eds.), *A dynamic approach to second language development: Methods and techniques* (pp. 5–24). John Benjamins Publishing. https://doi.org/10.1075/lllt.29.01deb.

de Bot, K., Lowie, W., & Verspoor, M. (2007). A dynamic view as a complementary perspective. *Bilingualism: Language and Cognition, 10*(01), 51–5. https://doi.org/10.1017/S1366728906002811.

Dmitrieva, O., Jongman, A., & Sereno, J. (2010). Phonological neutralization by native and non-native speakers: The case of Russian final devoicing. *Journal of Phonetics, 38*(3), 483–92. https://doi.org/10.1016/j.wocn.2010.06.001.

Dong, J. (2016). A dynamic systems theory approach to development of listening strategy use and listening performance. *System, 63,* 149–65. https://doi.org/10.1016/j.system.2016.10.004.

Eckman, F. R. (1981). On the naturalness of interlanguage phonological rules. *Language Learning, 31*(1), 195–216. https://doi.org/10.1111/j.1467-1770.1981.tb01379.x.

Escudero, P., & Williams, D. (2012). Native dialect influences second-language vowel perception: Peruvian versus Iberian Spanish learners of Dutch. *The Journal of the Acoustical Society of America, 131*(5), EL406–EL412. https://doi.org/10.1121/1.3701708.

Evans, D. R., & Larsen-Freeman, D. (2020). Bifurcations and the emergence of L2 syntactic structures in a Complex Dynamic System. *Frontiers in Psychology, 11,* 574603. https://doi.org/10.3389/fpsyg.2020.574603.

Faris, M. M., Best, C. T., & Tyler, M. D. (2016). An examination of the different ways that non-native phones may be perceptually assimilated as uncategorized. *The Journal of the Acoustical Society of America, 139*(1), EL1–EL5. https://doi.org/10.1121/1.4939608.

Flege, J. E. (1995). Second language speech learning: Theory, findings, and problems. In W. Strange (Ed.), *Speech perception and linguistic experience: Theoretical and methodological issues* (pp. 233–77). York Press.

Flege, J. E. (2002). Interactions between the native and second-language phonetic systems. In P. Burmeister, T. Piske & A. Rohde (Eds.), *An integrated view of language development: Papers in honor of Henning Wode* (pp. 217–44). Wissenschaftlicher Verlag.

Flege, J. E. (2003). Assessing constraints on second-language segmental production and perception. In N. O. Schiller & A. S. Meyer (Eds.), *Phonetics and phonology in language comprehension and production* (pp. 319–58). De Gruyter Mouton. https://doi.org/10.1515/9783110895094.319.

Flege, J. E., & Bohn, O.-S. (2021). The Revised Speech Learning Model (SLM-r). In R. Wayland (Ed.), *Second language speech learning* (1st ed., pp. 3–83). Cambridge University Press. https://doi.org/10.1017/9781108886901.002.

Flege, J. E., & Liu, S. (2001). The effect of experience on adults' acquisition of a second language. *Studies in Second Language Acquisition, 23*(4), 527–52. https://doi.org/10.1017/S0272263101004041.

Fowler, C. A. (1986). An event approach to the study of speech perception from a direct-realist perspective. *Journal of Phonetics, 14*(1), 3–28.

Gabriel, C., Kupisch, T., & Seoudy, J. (2016). VOT in French as a foreign language: A production and perception study with mono- and multilingual learners (German/Mandarin-Chinese). *SHS Web of Conferences, 27,* 1–14. https://doi.org/10.1051/shsconf/20162709002.

García Lecumberri, M., & Gallardo, F. (2003). English FL sounds in school learners of different ages. In M. del Pilar Garcia Mayo & M. Garcia Lecumberri (Eds.), *Age and the acquisition of English as a foreign language* (pp. 115–35). Multilingual Matters.

Gut, U. (2010). Cross-linguistic influence in L3 phonological acquisition. *International Journal of Multilingualism, 7*(1), 19–38. https://doi.org/10.1080/14790710902972248.

Hamann, S., & Sennema, A. (2005). Acoustic differences between German and Dutch labiodentals. *ZAS Papers in Linguistics, 42,* 33–41. https://doi.org/10.21248/zaspil.42.2005.272.

Hammarberg, B. (2017). Becoming multilingual: The macro and the micro time perspective. *International Review of Applied Linguistics in Language Teaching, 55*(1), 3–22. https://doi.org/10.1515/iral-2017-0010.

Hanulíková, A., van Alphen, P. M., van Goch, M. M., & Weber, A. (2012). When one person's mistake is another's standard usage: The effect of foreign accent on syntactic processing. *Journal of Cognitive Neuroscience, 24*(4), 878–87. https://doi.org/10.1162/jocn_a_00103.

Hillenbrand, J., Getty, L. A., Clark, M. J., & Wheeler, K. (1995). Acoustic characteristics of American English vowels. *The Journal of the Acoustical Society of America, 97*(5), 3099–111. https://doi.org/10.1121/1.411872.

Huang, T., Steinkrauss, R., & Verspoor, M. (2020). Learning an L2 and L3 at the same time: Help or hinder? *International Journal of Multilingualism, 19*(4), 566–82. https://doi.org/10.1080/14790718.2020.1779726.

Hufeisen, B. (2010). Theoretische Fundierung multiplen Sprachlernens – Faktorenmodell 2.0. *Jahrbuch Deutsch als Fremdsprache, 36*(1), 200–7.

Iverson, P., Ekanayake, D., Hamann, S., Sennema, A., & Evans, B. G. (2008). Category and perceptual interference in second-language phoneme learning: An examination of English /w/-/v/ learning by Sinhala, German, and Dutch speakers. *Journal of Experimental Psychology: Human Perception and Performance, 34*(5), 1305–16. https://doi.org/10.1037/0096-1523.34.5.1305.

Jassem, W. (2003). Polish. *Journal of the International Phonetic Association, 33*(1), 103–7. https://doi.org/10.1017/S0025100303001191.

Kohler, K. (1999). German. In *Handbook of the International Phonetic Association* (pp. 86–9). Cambridge University Press.

Kopečková, R. (2014). Crosslinguistic influence in instructed L3 child phonological acquisition. In M. Pawlak & L. Aronin (Eds.), *Essential topics in applied linguistics and multilingualism* (pp. 205–24). Springer International Publishing. https://doi.org/10.1007/978-3-319-01414-2_12.

Kopečková, R. (2016). The bilingual advantage in L3 learning: A developmental study of rhotic sounds. *International Journal of Multilingualism, 13*(4), 410–25. https://doi.org/10.1080/14790718.2016.1217605.

Kopečková, R., Marecka, M., Wrembel, M., & Gut, U. (2016). Interactions between three phonological subsystems of young multilinguals: The influence of language status. *International Journal of Multilingualism, 1*(4), 426. https://doi.org/10.1080/14790718.2016.1217603.

Lado, R. (1957). *Linguistics across cultures: Applied linguistics for language teachers*. University of Michigan Press. https://books.google.com/books?id=ZzYGAQAAIAAJ.

Larsen-Freeman, D. (2009). Adjusting expectations: The study of complexity, accuracy, and fluency in second language acquisition. *Applied Linguistics, 30* (4), 579–89. https://doi.org/10.1093/applin/amp043.

Larsen-Freeman, D., & Cameron, L. (2008). Research methodology on language development from a complex systems perspective. *The Modern Language Journal, 92*(2), 200–13. https://doi.org/10.1111/j.1540-4781.2008.00714.x.

Lima Jr., R. M. (2013). Complexity in second language phonology acquisition. *Revista Brasileira de Linguística Aplicada, 13*(2), 549–76.

Lima Jr., R. M., & Alves, U. K. (2019). A dynamic perspective on L2 pronunciation development: Bridging research and communicative teaching practice. *Revista do GEL, 16*(2), 27–56.

Llama, R., & Cardoso, W. (2018). Revisiting (non-)native influence in VOT production: Insights from advanced L3 Spanish. *Languages, 3*(3), 30. https://doi.org/10.3390/languages3030030.

Llama, R., Cardoso, W., & Collins, L. (2010). The influence of language distance and language status on the acquisition of L3 phonology. *International Journal of Multilingualism, 7*(1), 39–57. https://doi.org/10.1080/14790710902972255.

Llama, R., & López-Morelos, L. P. (2016). VOT production by Spanish heritage speakers in a trilingual context. *International Journal of Multilingualism, 13* (4), 444–58. https://doi.org/10.1080/14790718.2016.1217602.

Lowie, W. (2011). Early L2 phonology: A dynamic approach. In K. Dziubalska-Kołaczyk, M. Wrembel, & M. Kul (Eds.), *Proceedings of 6th New Sounds 2010* (pp. 159–70). Peter Lang.

Lowie, W. (2017). Lost in state space? Methodological considerations in Complex Dynamic Theory approaches to second language development research. In L. Ortega & Z. Han (Eds.), *Complexity theory and language development: In celebration of Diane Larsen-Freeman* (pp. 123–41). John Benjamins Publishing. https://doi.org/10.1075/lllt.48.07low.

Major, R. C. (2001). *Foreign accent: The ontogeny and phylogeny of second language phonology.* Lawrence Erlbaum.

Major, R. C. (2002). The phonology of the L2 user. In V. Cook (Ed.), *Portraits of the L2 user* (pp. 65–92). Multilingual Matters. https://books.google.de/books?id=FDmcuWKqmzwC&printsec=frontcover&hl=de&source=gbs_ge_summary_r&cad=0#v=onepage&q&f=false.

Morales Reyes, A., Arechabaleta-Regulez, B., & Montrul, S. A. (2017). The acquisition of rhotics by child L2 and L3 learners. *Journal of Second Language Pronunciation, 3*(2), 242–66. https://doi.org/10.1075/jslp.3.2.04rey.

Nagle, C. L. (2018). Examining the temporal structure of the perception-production link in second language acquisition: A longitudinal study. *Language Learning, 68*(1), 234–70. https://doi.org/10.1111/lang.12275.

Nelson, C. (2020). The younger, the better? Speech perception development in adolescent vs. adult L3 learners. *Yearbook of the Poznań Linguistic Meeting, 6*(1), 27–58. https://doi.org/10.2478/yplm-2020-0005.

Nelson, C. (2022). Do a learner's background languages change with increasing exposure to L3? Comparing the multilingual phonological development of adolescents and adults. *Languages, 7*(2), 78. https://doi.org/10.3390/languages7020078.

Pascoe, G. (1987). *Die Aussprache des Englischen an bayerischen Schulen: Untersuchungen an Gymnasien, Realschulen und Hauptschulen.* Profil.

Patience, M. (2018). Acquisition of the tap-trill contrast by L1 Mandarin–L2 English–L3 Spanish speakers. *Languages, 3*(4), 42. https://doi.org/10.3390/languages3040042.

Penris, W., & Verspoor, M. (2017). Academic writing development: A complex, dynamic process. In S. E. Pfenninger & J. Navracsics (Eds.), *Future research directions for applied linguistics* (pp. 215–42). Multilingual Matters.

Pfenninger, S. (2021). About the INTER and the INTRA in age-related research: Evidence from a longitudinal CLIL study with dense time serial measurements. *Linguistics Vanguard, 7*(2), 2020–8. https://doi.org/10.1515/lingvan-2020-0028.

Plonsky, L. (2015). Statistical power, *p* values, descriptive statistics, and effect sizes: A 'back-to-basics' approach to advancing quantitative methods in L2 research. In L. Plonsky (Ed.), *Advancing quantitative methods in second language research* (pp. 23–45). Routledge.

Plonsky, L., & Oswald, F. L. (2014). How big is 'big'? Interpreting effect sizes in L2 research. *Language Learning, 64*(4), 878–912. https://doi.org/10.1111/lang.12079.

Ribeiro, D. M. (2021). Third language acquisition: A study of unstressed vowel reduction. Doctoral thesis, Purdue University.

Roach, P. (2004). British English: Received pronunciation. *Journal of the International Phonetic Association, 34*(2), 239. https://doi.org/10.1017/S0025100304001768.

Rubach, J. (1984). *Cyclic and lexical phonology: The structure of Polish.* Foris Publications.

Sato, C. J. (1984). Phonological processes in second language acquisition: Another look at interlanguage syllable structure. *Language Learning, 34* (4), 43–58. https://doi.org/10.1111/j.1467-1770.1984.tb00351.x.

Saville-Troike, M. (2006). *Introducing second language acquisition.* Cambridge University Press.

Sharwood Smith, M. (1999). *Second language learning: Theoretical foundations* (4th ed.). Longman.

Shinohara, Y., Han, C., & Hestvik, A. (2019). Effects of perceptual assimilation: The perception of English /æ/, /ʌ/, AND /ɑ/ by Japanese speakers. In S. Calhoun, P. Escudero, M. Tabain, & P. Warren (Eds.), *Proceedings of the 19th International Congress of Phonetic Sciences* (pp. 603–8). Australasian Speech Science and Technology Association Inc.

Smith, B. L., Bruss, M., Hayes-Harb, R., & Hamilton, A. (2007). Voicing and devoicing in similar German and English word pairs by native speakers of German. *The Journal of the Acoustical Society of America, 122*(5), 3032. https://doi.org/10.1121/1.2942851.

Smith, B. L., & Peterson, E. A. (2012). Native English speakers learning German as a second language: Devoicing of word-final voiced stop targets. *The Journal of the Acoustical Society of America, 130*(4), 2523. https://doi.org/10.1121/1.3655068.

Spoelman, M., & Verspoor, M. (2010). Dynamic patterns in development of accuracy and complexity: A longitudinal case study in the acquisition of Finnish. *Applied Linguistics, 31*(4), 532–53. https://doi.org/10.1093/applin/amq001.

Stevens, K. N. (2000). *Acoustic phonetics.* MIT Press.

Strange, W., & Shafer, V. L. (2008). Speech perception in late second language learners: The re-education of selective perception. In J. G. Hansen & M. L. Zampini (Eds.), *Phonology and Second Language Acquisition* (pp. 153–191). John Benjamins Publishing.

Sypiańska, J. (2016). L1 vowels of multilinguals: The applicability of SLM in multilingualism. *Research in Language, 14*(1), 79–94. https://doi.org/10.1515/rela-2016-0003.

Sypiańska, J. (2017). Cross-linguistic influence in bilinguals and multilinguals. Doctoral thesis, Adam Mickiewicz University.

Traunmüller, H. (1990). *Analytical expressions for the tonotopic sensory scale. Journal of the Acoustical Society of America, 88*(1), 97–100. https://doi.org/10.1121/1.399849.

Taylor, W. E. (2021). *Change-Point Analyzer* 2.3 [Computer software]. https://variation.com.

Tyler, M. D. (2019). PAM-L2 and phonological category acquisition in the foreign language classroom. In A. M. Nyvad, M. Hejná, A. Højen, A. B. Jespersen, & M. H. Sørensen (Eds.), *A sound approach to language matters: In honor of Ocke-Schwen Bohn* (pp. 607–30). Aarhus University.

Tyler, M. D. (2021). Phonetic and phonological influences on the discrimination of non-native phones. In R. Wayland (Ed.), *Second language speech learning* (1st ed., pp. 157–74). Cambridge University Press. https://doi.org/10.1017/9781108886901.005.

van Dijk, M., & van Geert, P. (2007). Wobbles, humps and sudden jumps: A case study of continuity, discontinuity and variability in early language development. *Infant and Child Development, 16*(1), 7–33. https://doi.org/10.1002/icd.506.

van Dijk, M., Verspoor, M., & Lowie, W. (2011). Variability and DST. In M. Verspoor, K. de Bot, & W. Lowie (Eds.), *A dynamic approach to second language development: Methods and techniques* (pp. 55–84). John Benjamins Publishing. https://doi.org/10.1075/lllt.29.04van.

Verspoor, M., de Bot, K., & Lowie, W. (Eds.). (2011). *A dynamic approach to second language development: Methods and techniques.* John Benjamins Publishing.

Wrembel, M. (2014). VOT patterns in the acquisition of third language phonology. *Concordia Papers in Applied Linguistics, 5,* 751–71. http://repozytorium.amu.edu.pl:8080/bitstream/10593/12094/1/COPAL_paper_51-Wrembel%2C%20M.pdf.

Wrembel, M. (2015). Cross-linguistic influence in second vs. third language acquisition of phonology. In U. Gut, R. Fuchs, & E.-M. Wunder (Eds.), *Universal or diverse paths to English phonology* (pp. 41–70). De Gruyter Mouton. https://doi.org/10.1515/9783110346084-004.

Wrembel, M., Marecka, M., & Kopečková, R. (2019). Extending perceptual assimilation model to L3 phonological acquisition. *International Journal of Multilingualism, 16*(4), 513–33. https://doi.org/10.1080/14790718.2019.1583233

Yu, H., & Lowie, W. (2019). Dynamic paths of complexity and accuracy in second language speech: A longitudinal case study of Chinese learners. *Applied Linguistics, 41*(6), 855–77. https://doi.org/10.1093/applin/amz040.

Cambridge Elements ⁼

Phonetics

David Deterding
Universiti Brunei Darussalam

David Deterding is a Professor at Universiti Brunei Darussalam. His research has involved the measurement of rhythm, description of the pronunciation of English in Singapore, Brunei and China, and the phonetics of Austronesian languages such as Malay, Brunei Malay, and Dusun.

About the Series
The Cambridge Elements in Phonetics series will generate a range of high-quality scholarly works, offering researchers and students authoritative accounts of current knowledge and research in the various fields of phonetics. In addition, the series will provide detailed descriptions of research into the pronunciation of a range of languages and language varieties. There will be elements describing the phonetics of the major languages of the world, such as French, German, Chinese and Malay as well as the pronunciation of endangered languages, thus providing a valuable resource for documenting and preserving them.

Cambridge Elements ☰

Phonetics

Elements in the Series

The Phonetics of Malay
David Deterding, Ishamina Athirah Gardiner, Najib Noorashid

Spontaneous Speech
Benjamin V. Tucker, Yoichi Mukai

Phonetics and Phonology in Multilingual Language Development
Ulrike Gut, Romana Kopečková, Christina Nelson

A full series listing is available at: www.cambridge.org/EIPH

Printed in the United States
by Baker & Taylor Publisher Services